How to do a Research Project

How to do a Research Project
A Guide for Undergraduate Students

Colin Robson

Blackwell
Publishing

BLACKWELL PUBLISHING
350 Main Street, Malden, MA 02148-5020, USA
9600 Garsington Road, Oxford OX4 2DQ, UK
550 Swanston Street, Carlton, Victoria 3053, Australia

First published 2007 by Blackwell Publishing Ltd

1   2007

Library of Congress Cataloging-in-Publication Data

Robson, Colin
How to do a research project: a guide for undergraduate students / Colin Robson
p.   cm.
Includes bibliographical references and index.
ISBN-13: 978-1-4051-1489-9 (hardcover: alk. paper)
ISBN-10: 1-4051-1489-4 (hardcover: alk. paper)
ISBN-13: 978-1-4051-1490-5 (pbk.: alk. paper)
ISBN-10: 1-4051-1490-8 (pbk.: alk. paper)
1. Report writing. 2. Social sciences—Research. 3. Research—Methodology.
4. Project method in teaching. I. Title
LB2369.R575 2007
808'.0663—dc22
2006031104

A catalogue record for this title is available from the British Library.

Set in 10/12 pt Quadraat and Quadraat Sans
by The Running Head Limited, Cambridge, www.therunninghead.com
Printed and bound in Singapore
by Markono Print Media Pte Ltd

The publisher's policy is to use permanent paper from mills that operate a sustainable forestry policy,
and which has been manufactured from pulp processed using acid-free and elementary chlorine-
free practices. Furthermore, the publisher ensures that the text paper and cover board used have
met acceptable environmental accreditation standards.

For further information on
Blackwell Publishing, visit our website:
www.blackwellpublishing.com

Contents

Acknowledgements		xi
Introduction		1
Part I – Making Preparations		**5**
Project Planning Checklist		5
1	**Preliminaries**	**7**
	Recognizing Realities	7
	As a student on a course	*7*
	If you are by yourself	*7*
	If you are doing this as part of your job	*8*
	To everybody	*8*
	Making It Worthwhile	8
	Considering Your Audience(s)	9
	Individual or Group Research?	10
	Types of group research	*11*
	Support groups	*11*
	Working together successfully	*12*
	Project Milestones	12
	The Structure of the Book	14
	End-of-chapter Tasks	15
	Further Reading	15
	Chapter 1 Tasks	16
2	**Approaches to Research**	**18**
	A Concern for Truth	18
	Different Purposes of Research	19
	Description	*19*
	Exploration	*20*

Contents

Explanation	20
Emancipation	20
Research Design	21
The qualitative/quantitative divide	21
Fixed and flexible designs	22
Fixed designs	22
Flexible designs	22
Overview of Some Different Research Traditions	23
Action research	23
Case studies	26
Documentary analysis	28
Ethnographic research	30
Evaluation research	32
Experiments	35
Grounded theory studies	39
Surveys	41
A note on feminist research	44
Choosing an Approach	44
Further Reading	45
Chapter 2 Tasks	46
3 Developing Your Ideas	**47**
Selecting a Topic	47
Replication research	50
From a Topic to Research Questions	50
From Research Questions to a Research Design	51
Do I really need research questions?	52
Hypotheses	53
Developing the Design	53
Finding and Using Sources	54
Planning the search for sources	55
Internet searching	56
Library searching	61
Asking the author	62
Dealing with the sources	62
Ethical Considerations	64
Ethics committees	65
Ethical guidelines	66
Avoiding the unethical	66
Confirming Your Choices	67
Further Reading	67
Chapter 3 Tasks	69

4   Selecting the Method(s) of Collecting Data   70
       Trustworthiness and Credibility   71
          Reliability   *71*
          Validity   *72*
          Research arguments   *72*
       Data Collection Methods   73
       Interviews   73
          Fully structured interviews   *73*
          Semi-structured interviews   *74*
          Unstructured interviews   *75*
          Group interviews   *76*
          Telephone interviews   *77*
          Using interviews in your project   *78*
       Questionnaires and Diaries   79
          Questionnaires   *79*
          Diaries   *80*
          Using questionnaires or diaries in your project   *81*
       Tests and Scales   82
          Using tests or scales in your project   *83*
       Observation – Structured and Participant   84
          Structured observation   *84*
          Participant observation   *85*
          Using observation in your project   *86*
       Using Documents and Other Secondary Sources   88
          Library research   *90*
          Unobtrusive measures   *90*
          Using documents in your project   *91*
       Other Methods   91
       Using Multiple Methods   92
       Which Method?   92
       Further Reading   94
       Chapter 4 Tasks   94

Part II – Doing It   **95**

5   Practicalities of Data Collection   **97**
       Sampling and Sample Sizes   97
          Representative samples   *98*
          Non-probability samples   *99*
       Informed Consent   100
       Laboratory Research   100
       Gaining Access for Field Research   100

Contents

Formal and informal contracts	*103*
Getting on and getting out	*103*
Insider research	*104*
Pilots	105
Collecting the Data	106
What to Do if You Run into Difficulties or out of Time	107
Further Reading	108
Chapter 5 Tasks	109

Part III – Making Something of It — **113**

6 Analysing and Interpreting Your Findings 115

What This Chapter Tries to Do	115
Preparing for Analysis	116
Quantitative (Numerical) Data	117
Categorical variables	*117*
Ordered categorical variables	*118*
Summarizing and displaying categorical data	*119*
Continuous variables	*122*
Calculating summary statistics with continuous variables	*123*
Calculating variability	*124*
Displaying continuous variables	*125*
Statistical tests and statistical significance	*125*
Effect sizes	*126*
Clinical significance	*127*
What test do I use?	*127*
Qualitative Data	130
Data reduction and organization	*130*
An example – the grounded theory approach to analysis	*132*
Using specialist computer packages for qualitative data analysis	*133*
Summary of qualitative data analysis	*134*
Interpretation – What Is Going on Here?	135
Further Reading	137
Chapter 6 Tasks	138

7 Writing the Report 139

Planning and Drafting	140
Research Arguments	142
Claims	*143*
Reasons and evidence	*143*

Considering Your Audience(s) Again   145
Avoiding Plagiarism   146
Professional Standards   146
  Language matters   147
  References   147
  Abstracts and executive summaries   148
The First Full Draft   148
Revising and Polishing   149
The Final Version   150
Other Forms of Presentation   150
A Final Word   151
Further Reading   151
Chapter 7 Tasks   152

References and Author Index   153
Subject Index   155

Acknowledgements

I am very grateful to the many students and colleagues at Birkbeck College, University of London, the University of Huddersfield, and the former Hester Adrian Research Centre, University of Manchester, who have, in various ways, contributed to my education as a writer. I give particular thanks to the late Professor Brian Foss who, many years ago, encouraged me to turn lecture notes prepared for University of London Summer Schools in Experimental Psychology into a text on research design, which first set me on the writing route.

In the preparation of this book I would particularly like to acknowledge help and advice from Maximilian Forte, Department of Sociology and Anthropology, Concordia University, Montreal; Kate Gerrish, School of Nursing and Midwifery, University of Sheffield; Graham Gibbs, Behavioural Sciences Department, University of Huddersfield; Paul Oliver, School of Education and Professional Development, University of Huddersfield; and Penny Renwick, School of Health, Psychology and Social Care, Manchester Metropolitan University. Also to the three anonymous reviewers for Blackwell whose helpful and insightful comments helped me to sort out several omissions and confusions in an earlier draft. I continue to find working with colleagues from Blackwell a totally positive experience, and would like to give particular mention to the help and advice given by Sarah Bird in the early stages of the development of this book, and to Elizabeth-Ann Johnston who has ably taken up the reins following Sarah's departure to fresh fields.

Emma Place and Caroline Williams, of Intute, and Debra Hiom of Intute: Social Sciences based at the Universities of Manchester and Bristol, generously gave their time, and shared their plans for the development of these absolutely invaluable internet resources (discussed in chapter 3 of the book). I am also grateful for formal agreement to incorporate material from the Intute Virtual

Training Suite on 'Social Research Methods' (www.vts.intute.ac.uk), written by Louise Corti of the Department of Sociology and Data Archive, University of Essex, as Box 3.4.

I would also like to put on record, on behalf of anyone doing a research project, thanks for the wealth of useful material now freely available on the Web. Sites such as Bill Trochim's 'Web Center for Social Research Methods' (www.socialresearchmethods.net/) and the 'Social Science Undergraduate Dissertation Companion' (www.socscidiss.bham.ac.uk/) edited by Malcolm Todd from Sheffield Hallam University, are examples to us all.

As ever, I am indebted to my wife Pat for, among many other things, her sage advice on written style. It is probably too late for me to learn the finer points of comma and semi-colon placement, but she sorts this out very patiently.

Finally, I owe a debt of gratitude to Wayne Booth, Gregory Colomb and Joseph Williams whose book *The Craft of Research* (University of Chicago Press, 2nd edition, 2003) provided an inspirational model of how a student-oriented text can give advice and support over a wide range of disciplines. I could not hope to emulate the clarity and precision of presentation which they, as specialists in English language and literature, bring. But they have shown what is possible.

Introduction

This book covers the things you need to think about when carrying out the research project that forms an important part of many undergraduate degree courses. The focus is on disciplines and areas where the methods of social research are used. It concentrates on the issues involved and on the range of possibilities you might consider.

There is a general checklist of the things you will need to cover when planning the project on page 5. Extensive annotated lists of further reading are included at the end of each chapter and in other places. I have also incorporated substantial amounts of additional material in the website associated with the book (www.blackwellpublishing.com/researchproject).

This website includes references to specific research issues, and relevant examples of research in social science disciplines and applied fields where the methods of social research are commonly used, including:

- [ ] business and management studies
- [ ] education
- [ ] nursing and other health-related areas
- [ ] psychology
- [ ] social anthropology
- [ ] social work and social policy
- [ ] sociology, and
- [ ] sport and leisure studies.

The book should also be useful to students taking courses in other fields, who wish to carry out projects calling for the use of these methods, e.g. in architecture, art and design, catering and hospitality studies, communications and journalism, computer sciences, conflict and peace studies, criminology, development studies, environmental studies, geography, history, information sciences, legal studies, literary studies, media studies, medicine, music, planning, political science, religious studies, tourism, and urban design.

The material in the book itself focuses on what you need to make decisions about the various aspects of your research project. The website and the suggested supplementary readings are designed to provide the information needed for you to act on those decisions.

My hope and intention is to give help and advice to students carrying out this type of research project. This book will, I hope, be of practical value in many areas of research. It concentrates on research where the focus is on people, what they do and how we can understand what is going on. My own background is as a psychologist, working mainly in applied fields such as education and health-related areas. However, the basics of doing research using social research methods seem to me to have many characteristics in common, whatever the field. What do differ from field to field are the expectations, assumptions and traditions of researchers. While you will need to take note of this (discussed under the heading of 'Considering your audience(s)' in chapter 1, p. 9, and chapter 7, p. 145), the first-time researcher can bring to the task freshness of vision and absence of preconceptions.

The focus is on small-scale research – typically the 'final year' project which forms an important part of many degree courses, often with preparatory sessions at the end of the previous year.

My aim is to give you the confidence to complete a worthwhile project. This need not be a very difficult technical task, but it does call for:

☐ *organization* (sorting out what you have to do)
☐ *commitment* (actually doing it) and, almost always,
☐ *good social skills* (getting on with people, not upsetting them or getting their backs up).

I share the belief of Wayne Booth and his colleagues Gregory Colomb and Joseph Williams, expressed in their text *The Craft of Research* (Booth et al., 2003), that 'the skills of doing and reporting research are not just for the elite; they can be learned by all students' (p. xii).

All projects must fulfil two crucial criteria. Firstly, that they are *feasible*. They can be completed with the resources, including time, that you have available (see chapter 5, p. 97). Secondly, that they are *ethical*. The project will not cause harm to those involved or others (see chapter 3, p. 64).

Research depends on getting hold of some information or data and doing something with it. A central message of this book is that the type of information or data you need to collect is largely determined by the questions to which you seek answers – known, unsurprisingly, as the *research questions*. Sorting this out is the main task in chapter 3.

There are some suggestions for further reading at the end of each chapter, and at the end of sections on different approaches to doing research in chapter 2, and on different methods of data collection in chapter 4. They are annotated with short descriptions of what you might get from each one. I've tried to select, whenever possible, up-to-date books which are readily available and not hideously expensive.

The website associated with the text also includes links to useful websites and references to articles in academic and professional journals available as e-journals (i.e. journals which are available electronically as well as, or instead of, a paper version). Wherever possible, they are from open access journals or from those likely to be accessible via academic libraries. The Web is an absolutely invaluable resource for anyone doing research (see chapter 3, p. 56), although you need to check the quality of the information source as discussed in that chapter.

A note on gender and language

To avoid giving the impression that all researchers and others mentioned are female (or male), and disliking the 'she/he' approach, I use the plural 'they' whenever possible. If the singular can't be avoided, I use 'he' and 'she' more or less randomly.

Part I

Making Preparations

Project Planning Checklist

1 Know the rules
2 Decide on a topic
3 Read and talk
4 Decide on the research questions
5 Decide on the design
6 Consider ethical issues
7 Obtain any necessary approvals for access
8 Draw up a project outline and timetable.

Before committing yourself, you need to know the realities of your situation. What kind of project is expected? What kind of report? When is the deadline? See chapter 1, pages 7–8.

If your topic hasn't been decided for you, and if you don't already have a topic in mind, possible topics should be discussed with your supervisor and others who might help. See chapter 3, pages 47–50.

Use sources of information (people, books, journals, internet, etc.) to confirm, or change, your choice of topic. See chapter 3, pages 54–62.

Note: You will also have to use sources when sorting out each of the following topics.

1 Come up with a small number of questions to which your research will plan to produce answers. These questions may be modified as you get further into the research process. See chapter 3, pages 50–3.
2 Consider what general approach, and which method or methods of data collection, will provide answers to these questions. See chapter 2, pages 23–44 (approaches) and chapter 4, pages 73–92 (methods).
3 Evaluate the ethical issues arising from your proposed research and work out how they will be dealt with. See chapter 3, pages 64–7.
4 Seek approval, at the earliest possible date, from whoever is responsible. See chapter 5, pages 100–3.
5 List all the stages which you need to go through to do the research and end up with a completed project report. Produce a realistic timetable. See chapter 5, pages 109–11.

This first part covers the things that you need to think about, and get sorted out, before carrying out your project. Doing a research project is rather like house painting and decorating – prepare thoroughly and you reap the rewards when doing the job.

The project planning checklist lists the main things you need to consider. The following chapters discuss the issues involved in detail. There is a set of tasks at the end of each chapter to help you plan.

1

Preliminaries

Recognizing Realities

The realities of your situation will strongly influence what you can do. For example:

As a student on a course

☐ *What are the course requirements?* You need to know the formal specification for the research project. Things like the type of project expected; how and when it is to be presented – length, format, etc. The general rule is – if they say 'these are the rules', then you follow them. There may be room for negotiation or interpretation if you feel that some aspect isn't appropriate for the project you want to do – but you must get this agreed before proceeding.

☐ *What are the expectations of your tutor or supervisor?* To become supervisors people have to be fully qualified and professionally competent. They are your best guide to the development and completion of a successful project. Supervisors are human beings and as such will have their own preferences, expectations and even prejudices about what makes a good project. While the obvious strategy is to go along with them, the good supervisor should welcome your initiative if you come up with reasoned proposals for doing it somewhat differently. If they are not amenable to your suggested approach, do remember that the supervisor has substantially more experience than you. It is politic to follow their suggestions. With the experience of completing this project behind you, you will be in a better position to decide for yourself when you do your next piece of research.

If you are by yourself

☐ *Can you get help?* This book will provide support to a lone novice researcher. However it is highly desirable that you find someone to give advice and support, and to bounce ideas off.

One strategy is to sign up as a student at a local college or through the internet. This should get you supervisory support and access to an academic library (and through this to a wide range of Web resources), but the course requirements may set an inappropriate straitjacket on the kind of project you can do. It may also mean that you have to do additional courses which, while they could well assist in you doing a better project, may not fit in with your plans.

If you are doing this as part of your job (whether or not on a course)

☐ *What is the expectation within your organization?* You may be doing this project because your boss or line manager has asked you to. This puts you in a strong position because it is in their interest to give you the support needed to enable you to do the job. You need to know why they want the work done, mainly so that you can frame the project in such a way that it stands a chance of answering their questions. But it is also so that you can satisfy yourself you aren't being asked to do something unethical (see 'Avoiding the unethical', chapter 3, p. 66).

Much research by practitioners, whether focusing on their own organization or a different one, concerns meeting perceived needs – of the organization, its clients, customers or users, of workers within the organization, or more widely of the community or area it serves. This has the advantage of helping to justify asking people to give their time to contribute to the project. It also makes them more likely to be involved if it is seen to be trying to meet these needs. It does mean, however, that you have to spend time and effort on finding out about such needs and, perhaps, of reconciling the different needs of different groups.

To everybody

One of the commonest problems of novice researchers (and of experienced ones who should know better) is biting off more than they can chew. They under-estimate how long things take and over-estimate what they can do with the time and resources that they have available. Be warned.

Making It Worthwhile

Two main things make doing a research project worthwhile for you. Firstly, completing it. Secondly, the skills and experience you gain from doing it. Completing it (which includes writing a report) helps justify the time and effort that you have put into it. An unfinished project means that you have effectively wasted the time of the people who have taken part, including yourself.

Doing a research project calls for a wide range of skills and gives valuable experience. These include:

☐ *process skills* – such as problem formulation and solving, use of data collection techniques, data analysis, etc.
☐ *presentation skills* – such as report writing, data presentation, audience awareness, etc.
☐ *management skills* – such as project planning, time management, working with others, etc., and
☐ *personal skills* – such as self-discipline, originality, ability to learn, acceptance of criticism, etc.

All of these can, of course, be made much of on your résumé or CV.

A successfully completed project puts you in the position to do better and bigger further projects. It is not uncommon for doctoral and other postgraduate research to have its roots in this first small-scale project. Mistakes and blunders can provide useful learning experiences. They will be etched on your mind, making their repetition highly unlikely (you will just make different mistakes – nobody is perfect!).

Practitioners making a good job of a project are likely to be asked to do more, leading perhaps to a formal research role in their organization. Moreover, the skills acquired can be transferred into other contexts. Many tasks, other than purely routine ones, for those dealing with people as part of their job, involve the central research activities of planning, information or data gathering, analysis and reporting.

Be wary of using people as 'research-fodder'. If people take part in your project and give you time and attention, you should seek to *make it worthwhile for the participants in the project*. This can be through:

☐ *Giving feedback* The deal you agree when asking others to take part in your project (see chapter 5, pp. 101–3) should normally involve you undertaking to let them know something about your findings.
☐ *Letting them talk* People are often pleased by someone showing an interest in them and relish the opportunity of talking to an interested person about themselves. So, don't just cut and run when you have what you need for the project. It is not unknown for their spontaneous comments to be more interesting than the answers to your carefully crafted questions.

Considering Your Audience(s)

In one sense, you carry out the research for yourself. Perhaps because you want to find out or understand something. Or because it will help you gain a qualification, or further your career. However, other people come into the picture. You can think of them as audiences for your research. This is most obvious in relation to the report you will produce. If the project is for an award, then your examiners are a crucial audience. There will be a formal specification and you must make sure that you know what this is and stick to it. If it says 10,000 words, you stay very close to that limit.

Much social research carries with it the notion, implicitly or explicitly, that by carrying it out, you might help to change and improve some situation. This has implications for both the content and style of your report. Something written for a senior management team in a business will differ from a report seeking to communicate to volunteers at a centre for young persons with learning difficulties. These issues are returned to in the final chapter.

However, bearing audience in mind is important at all stages of the project. When doing research as part of a formal qualification, your supervisor forms an audience you want to please. They will have views and prejudices to take note of. If you are doing the research as part of your job, it is essential that you find out what your boss or line manager is expecting from the project. And that you plan something which will deliver this (or indulge in a subtle re-education process where you persuade that there is a better way).

To get the active support that you need to carry out a successful project in an organization, it will help not only to have the top brass on your side, but also to be doing something that is potentially helpful to the lower echelons (see the section on gaining access in chapter 5). More generally, whoever act as participants in your study constitute an audience to take note of. Your interactions with them should show respect and consideration for their likely sensitivities.

Considering these multiple audiences influences the nature of your project. Some audiences only respect quantitative, statistical evidence. Others would take more note of rich qualitative data. If you have to satisfy both kinds of audience, you might have to use more than one method or approach, and possibly produce different reports for them.

Individual or Group Research?

There is much to be said in favour of collaborating with others when carrying out a research project. Research is very commonly a group activity, and demonstrating that you have acquired the skills of working with others is another marketable asset. However, some degree course regulations either insist on individual projects or set strict limits on the type of collaboration that is allowed. Check this out.

Types of group research

Group research can take many forms:

☐ Forming a group with fellow students or colleagues where the research is jointly designed, carried out and reported on. Decisions are reached via consensus. It is not an easy option and is very risky unless you and the other group members have already got successful experience of working in this way. This approach is commonly not permitted by course regulations, in part because of the difficulty in assessing the individual contributions of group members.
☐ Forming a group where several people are interested in the same broad topic and, through discussion, carve out related projects. Details of the design and other aspects of each project are the responsibility of the individual concerned, with other members of the group giving advice and support at all stages. The quality of your project is likely to be enhanced by linking the discussion and findings to those of other group members. Providing that you clearly signal which parts are your own work and which that of others, it would be unreasonable for course regulations to prohibit this form of group working.
☐ Forming a group with persons having a role in the setting where your research takes place. This applies particularly when your project involves evaluating a programme, intervention, innovation, or whatever, where there is much advantage in involving the personnel concerned. For example, a project that is focused on problems and issues that they feel are important, is much more likely to get their active co-operation than trying to persuade them to go along with your own pet ideas (see Robson, 2000; chapter 2, for more details about the advantages of this kind of collaboration in evaluations).

Support groups

Even when everyone wants to do their own thing, and the proposed topics are very various, forming a mutual support group is well worthwhile. Group members will have different strengths and perspectives, and will be able to offer comments. Toward the completion of the project, reading of each other's draft reports is very valuable. It is a good idea to agree ground rules for the group at an early stage (e.g. criticism and comments to be constructive; attendance at meetings is a priority; feedback on drafts and other materials to be within one week, etc.). See also the following section 'Working together successfully'.

Supervisor support If, for whatever reasons, you decide to do an individual project, this is fine. Most people do. As already stressed (p. 7), for anyone on a course, your supervisor is a major resource. Teachers want their students to succeed (partly, though hopefully not solely, because it can take a lot of their effort to help get an unsatisfactory project up to standard). If you are not getting the support you are entitled to, there should be mechanisms for remedying the situation. Be reasonable though. They are busy people and you have your part of the bargain to fulfil through attendance and involvement.

Web-based discussion and other groups You could also consider ways of getting involved in, or forming, a group via the Web. There is a very large number of discussion groups and other Web entities through which you can get advice, and possibly also get in touch with persons in a similar situation as yourself. I have been very impressed by the way in which established researchers are willing to give advice to those less experienced, in discussion groups on a wide range of research-related topics. The usual warnings and safeguards about Web activities apply (see chapter 3, p. 56).

Working together successfully

Booth, Colomb and Williams' Chicago Guide to Writing, Editing and Publishing (Booth et al., 2003) though focused mainly on research in the humanities, provides helpful advice on group working relevant to all novice researchers. Their 'keys for working together successfully' include:

☐ *Talk a lot.* They advise setting up conditions which get you talking a lot, through regular meetings, exchanging e-mails, etc. I was particularly taken by their notion that you concentrate first on your 'elevator story' (to a UK English audience perhaps a 'lift tale'). This is how you would describe your project to a stranger in the time it takes to get from the first to the twentieth floor. Polish this at all opportunities so that it sounds convincing both to yourself and others.

☐ *Agree to disagree.* You are bound to disagree about some things, but try to keep these disagreements in perspective.

☐ *Organize and plan.* Appoint a co-ordinator (facilitator, moderator, organizer if you prefer). Decide whether the role rotates or stays with the same person. It's their job to keep the group on track, through calling meetings, checking progress, moderating discussions, etc. (pp. 27–8).

Project Milestones

Box 1.1 sets out the key elements of a project. It sounds pretty straightforward. In many ways it is, but hidden beneath the surface there are many things you need to consider.

It is self-evident that you need to sort out a *focus* or topic for your project. The 'questions to which you are seeking answers' are the *research questions* which

Box 1.1 Project milestones

Deciding:
1 **The focus of your research**
2 **The question(s) to which you are seeking answers**
3 **The ways of getting the answers**

then:

4 *Seeking* **the answers**

and finally:

5 *Telling* **others what you have found.**

have already been referred to. Coming up with a set of non-trivial questions, which are answerable given the time and resources you have available, is a very useful way of giving a shape to your efforts. It also helps if you are clear about what you hope to achieve by doing the research – its *purpose*. You will find it argued in some texts that the purpose of research is to provide explanations, but very worthwhile research can be mainly concerned with exploration or description.

The 'ways of getting answers' to these research questions are the *research methods*, such as questionnaires, interviews, observation, documentary analysis, etc., which you decide to use.

However, 'ways of getting answers' also refers to the overall approach to research which is selected. There are very different *styles, or strategies, of research* ranging from a tightly controlled experimental design collecting quantitative (numerical) data, to ethnographic approaches relying on participant observation and producing largely qualitative (non-numerical, usually verbal) data.

'Seeking the answers' moves on to actual *data or information collection*. Reliance on existing information (sometimes referred to as documentary analysis, or library research) is a fully legitimate form of research activity, and is the norm in some fields or discipline. However, much research involves active data collection (sometimes referred to as primary data collection), whether inside or outside a specialist laboratory. Non-laboratory, or 'field' research, has its own challenges which often call for good social skills, as well as skills in using the research methods.

'Telling others what you have found' is *writing a report*, which is the essential culmination of the whole exercise. However, before you can write the report, you need to know what you have found. Collected data typically do not speak for themselves. You have to make them talk. This process of achieving understanding of what you have found through *analysis and interpretation* is often presented as difficult and highly technical. It can be, and you may need specialist help, but often a simple analysis is preferable.

The Structure of the Book

The book is in three parts. The first covers the things you need to get sorted out in advance. The second covers practical aspects of collecting your data. The final part discusses what to do with the data when you have collected them.*

In Part I, following the preliminaries discussed in this first chapter:

- ☐ Chapter 2 tries to help you appreciate some possible approaches to research.
- ☐ Chapter 3 is concerned with selecting a topic and getting you to the stage where you have an initial set of research questions; then deciding what overall style of research will be best fitted to get you answers.
- ☐ Chapter 4 reviews a range of methods you might consider to collect data; then how to choose the one(s) for your project.

Part II is:

- ☐ Chapter 5 and covers the practicalities of actually collecting data.

In Part III:

- ☐ Chapter 6 focuses on what to do with the data, and
- ☐ Chapter 7 deals with report writing.

This is, I hope, a logical, and understandable, sequence. However, it may give the mistaken impression that research is a tidy, essentially linear, process where one moves through the various stages and the report pops out at the end. In practice, it is often much more messy and interactive than this. You may find that there are constraints or limitations on what is possible, which crop up at a late stage and force you to change tack. Or, an opportunity to do something different comes out of the blue. Your reading, or discussions with colleagues or a supervisor, or what you get from participants, may make you realize that what you had proposed was wrong-headed. Pilot studies may reveal that you have grossly under-estimated the time things take, etc. (see chapter 5, p. 105)

Specific 'non-linear' aspects to consider include:

---

* Strictly speaking 'data' are plural – the singular is 'datum'. However it is often treated as a singular noun. I prefer the plural, but it's up to you.

☐ Being prepared to revisit your initial research questions and revise them in the light of the way things are turning out. At one extreme you may find, toward the end, that you have found answers to different questions! Be grateful for such mercies.

☐ Sorting out any arrangements for access and ethical clearance as soon as you are reasonably certain of the nature and design of your project.

☐ Ensuring that your design is such that you will be able to carry out any analyses you need to do (e.g. that sample sizes are large enough for particular statistical tests to be possible). This means that you need to know how the data will be analysed before they are collected.

☐ Starting writing at an early stage. Don't leave it all to the end. Drafts of substantial chunks can be done along the way. Many potentially high quality projects are ruined by a mad scramble to complete the analysis and the report, trying to meet what has become an impossibly tight deadline.

End-of-chapter Tasks

Each of the chapters is followed by a set of tasks. These are suggestions about things to do, arising from the material covered in that chapter. Whether you complete all, or even any of them, is obviously up to you. My recommendation is that you:

☐ *Start the chapter 1 tasks now*, or at least as soon as practicable.

☐ *Then read through the whole of the book* so that you get a feel for all aspects of completing the project. Don't worry at this stage if you don't understand everything. Note the tasks and perhaps give some preliminary thoughts about what you might do, but don't actually complete them.

☐ *Return to the beginning and*, working in 'real time' (i.e. the time dictated by the requirements of the project) *go through the chapter tasks* broadly in sequence, rereading material in the chapter as necessary. It may make sense to combine tasks for different chapters depending on how things work out.

Further Reading

Robson, C. (2002) *Real World Research: A resource for social scientists and practitioner-researchers*. 2nd edition. Oxford: Blackwell. A big book. It takes the same general approach as this text but goes into considerably greater detail at a somewhat higher level. Use it for following up specific aspects relevant to your project, or if you feel the need for additional background on doing research.

Chapter 1 Tasks

1 *Get a project diary.* This is a notebook in which you enter a variety of things relevant to the project. It can take many different forms but I like to have a nice quality one with hardback covers and not just a loose-leaf writing pad. I suspect that, psychologically, if you have invested in something like this, it gives an added impetus to keeping a quality record. Who knows, it might be the start of your career library of project diaries. An alternative is to have the equivalent of this diary on your computer (make sure you keep back-ups). The kinds of things which might be entered into your diary include:

- ☐ notes of all meetings and data collection sessions relating to the project – particularly of meetings with a supervisor. If the data, or full notes are somewhere else, give details of where they are.
- ☐ appointments made, and kept
- ☐ notes from library, internet and other information-gathering sessions
- ☐ memos to yourself about any aspect of the project – what you are proposing to do and why
- ☐ notes about the modification of earlier intentions and why they are made
- ☐ responses to the later tasks in the book
- ☐ reminders of things to be done, people to be chased up, etc.
- ☐ taking stock of where you are; short interim reports of progress, problems and worries; memos to yourself of bright thoughts you have had (get it down before you forget!), suggestions for what might be done.

The diary can be invaluable when you get to the stage of putting together the findings of the project and writing the report. It acts as a memory jogger, and an invaluable brake on any tendencies to rewrite history. It is, in itself, a learning tool for future research projects.

2 *Start using it.* In particular it will be useful if you can write down a short account of your initial thoughts about the project you are hoping to do (don't worry if you are not at all sure at this stage – it's what you do by the end that counts). Half a page, or so, is enough. There is a lot to be said in favour of doing this before reading further as it will then be possible for you to look at it later, and gain insights into how far you have travelled in the process of doing the project.

3 *Investigate possibilities for collaboration.* If the idea of carrying out your project on some kind of group basis interests you, then now is the time to find out what may be possible:

☐ Is it allowed? Are there regulations or rules that forbid group work – or particular kinds of group work? Find out.

☐ Are there other students you could work with? If so, get together and sort out what kind of group you can agree on. Get started by sharing ideas on what topic(s) you might go for.

Even if a group project of some kind is not possible, for whatever reason, everyone can benefit from being part of a *support group*. Set one up now.

2

Approaches to Research

This chapter gives an overview of several widely used general approaches to carrying out research in the social sciences and other related fields. It also sets out different purposes that a research project might have. The intention is that, before you get down to developing your ideas about what your own project might look like, you appreciate something of the range of possibilities.

If you already have a good idea about both the topic you want to focus on, and the approach to take (perhaps you are in the fortunate position that your supervisor has provided you with a list of topics together with a strong steer about approach), reading this chapter is still worthwhile. An appreciation of the range of possible approaches can give you a better feel for why you are doing what you are doing. And whatever research approach you use, it is important to take on board the 'concern for truth' discussed in the next section.

Unless you have had the choice of approach decided for you, try to avoid early closure. You may be pretty convinced at this stage that you are going to carry out a survey of some kind. Try to suspend judgement until you have considered different possibilities. Follow up any that interest you and/or seem likely to be appropriate for your project.

First, some general guidelines for everyone starting on the research quest.

A Concern for Truth

Research tries to get at the 'truth'. The scare quotes around 'truth' indicate that philosophers have difficulty deciding what it means – and how we would know when, or if, we had found it. For our purposes it's best to contrast it with what you should not be doing. You are not out to 'sell' something. You are not just seeking evidence to push some particular line, or to support some pet notion or theory.

This can get difficult. You don't stop being a human being when you do research. You are likely to come to any topic with pre-existing views, particularly if you choose something that interests you (which is a very sensible thing to do – see chapter 3, p. 47). Researchers inevitably bring their values and opinions with them when researching. The task is to work at making sure that this doesn't bias the research.

It boils down to working:

☐ *systematically* – where you have given serious thought to what you are doing and how you are going to do it
☐ *sceptically* – where you challenge your ideas and findings, and get others to do the same (have you really justified what you are claiming, have you considered alternatives?), and
☐ *ethically* – where you seek to ensure that you are not harming those taking part in the research, or who might be affected by it. And where you don't pass off other people's work as your own, or invent data.

Following these guidelines can go a long way toward helping you carry out a simple project. In many fields there will be specialist expertise you need to acquire to produce something credible. And, in just about all fields, there is now a substantial tradition of ways in which research has been done.

Different Purposes of Research

In trying to home in on a specific project, it helps if you can clarify what you see as the central purpose of your research. Some claim that the only acceptable purpose of doing research is to provide an explanation of some phenomenon. I would argue that, particularly in the field of social research, worthwhile research can focus on describing something. Or on conducting an exploration of some little-known phenomenon. Many social researchers would also maintain that there is a responsibility on the part of the researcher to seek to improve the lot of those who get a raw deal in society, i.e. that research could and should have an emancipatory function.

Description

Description is sometimes regarded as too mundane a purpose to qualify as research. Some descriptions are undoubtedly so trivial that they are clearly not worthy of the name. However, a descriptive study carried out with the 'systematically, sceptically and ethically' hallmarks discussed above, and which provides answers to a well thought through set of research questions, could be of real value.

Exploration

There are, similarly, researchers who look down their noses at an exploratory study. Nothing but a fishing trip! In new and poorly understood areas, exploration could well be the most useful tactic. It is the quality of the work that should determine its research status rather than the purpose.

Explanation

The above arguments for taking a broad church view of research purposes should not be taken as denying the importance of explanatory research. It could be reasonably argued that there is some kind of hierarchy, where description and exploration provide necessary precursors to the task of providing explanations of what is going on in some researched situation.

In simple terms, we have an explanation when we have a good idea about 'what is going on' in the situation we are researching. Perhaps we recognize that it is an example of a particular type of situation, or that some existing theory applies, or needs modifying, or developing, to account for what we have found.

One way of looking at this that you may find helpful is to think in terms of mechanisms. This is common in biological and medical research. For example, there have been press reports that 'scientists think that they are unravelling the secret of just why greens are good for you in the fight against cancer'. This is because they have been able to move from descriptive studies based on studying cancer rates between different populations with different diets, to an understanding of the specific mechanism through which chemicals in some brassica vegetables prevent pre-cancerous cells turning into potentially deadly cancer cells.

The approach is now being used in social research. See, for example, studies discussed in Pawson and Tilley (1997) of the likely mechanisms at work in reducing car park crime by the use of closed circuit television (pp. 78–82). This topic is returned to in discussing the interpretation of your findings (chapter 6, p. 135).

Emancipation

Here the purpose is to empower relatively powerless groups (such as women, minorities, or persons with disabilities). This has been a strong theme in much feminist research. It involves a study not only of their lives and experiences, but also of how oppressors maintain their dominance. Research can play an important role in anti-discrimination agenda and in promoting user involvement and user voices in services and more generally. One of the complexities of research with an emancipatory purpose is that the (relatively powerful) researcher is called upon to relinquish this power to the marginalized group.

Research Design

'Design deals primarily with aims, uses, purposes, intentions and plans' (Hakim, 1987; p. 1). Hakim also stresses its concern with practical constraints set by the resources available, and that it is very much about style. She makes an analogy with the role of the architect in building design. Houses can be erected by builders without benefit of an architect, and can provide an awful warning. You can build your research project simply by following one or more of the standard research methods. However, by giving thought to the overall design of your project (and of how a particular research method, such as using questionnaires, fits into it), you are more likely to end up with something fit for its purpose.

The qualitative/quantitative divide

You are likely to find, in further reading and elsewhere, discussions on 'qualitative research' and 'quantitative research'. Qualitative research is an umbrella term covering several different research traditions which have in common a reliance on the collection of qualitative data, usually, though not necessarily, in the form of words. The tradition has arisen, in part as a reaction against approaches such as experimentation and survey work, which not only rely almost exclusively on quantitative, numerical, data, but also often claim the research high ground as generating the only kind of reliable scientific data.

The counter argument is that in social research, where one seeks to understand people and their ways, numbers and statistical analyses are of little real value. While these qualitative versus quantitative wars are still fought by die-hards on each side, it is increasingly recognized that such absolutist positions are unhelpful. In disciplines such as psychology, formerly largely occupied by experimentalists, there is increasing interest in the use of qualitative approaches.

It is generally appreciated that there are certain questions best dealt with by approaches yielding 'hard' numerical data, others by ones generating 'soft' qualitative data. And that, depending on the questions to which you seek answers, there can be advantages in incorporating both the qualitative and the quantitative in the same study. To avoid the rather stale conflict between qualitative and quantitative camps, I find it useful to talk in terms of fixed and flexible designs.

Fixed and flexible designs

The approaches discussed below illustrate different styles of doing research, ranging from the relatively safe and conventional to the more adventurous. They can be loosely grouped into two broad families – *fixed designs*, where the design is largely pre-specified and sorted out in detail before the main collection of data takes place, and *flexible designs*, where things are much more fluid. Here, the way in which the research proceeds depends on the initial findings. Hence the details of the design, rather than being largely pre-specified, emerge during the process of the project.

Fixed designs

In these designs there may be some preliminary data collection at an early stage to test out ideas to see whether they are practical. Such piloting is indeed highly desirable (see chapter 5, p. 105). However, this style requires you to have worked out in advance a detailed plan of what you are going to do before you start the main data collection. Of the approaches considered in this chapter, surveys and experiments are the classic examples of fixed design research. Some forms of evaluation research and, more unusually, of documentary analysis also follow fixed design principles.

Flexible designs

With flexible designs you still have to do some preliminary work to sort out the focus of your research and the general approach you will be taking. Also you will have initial ideas about the research questions to which you will be seeking answers. However, you start the data collection in earnest at a much earlier stage of preparation than in fixed design research. With this style, decisions about how to proceed depend to a considerable extent on what you find out from the early data collection. Hence the design evolves. You might change tack to follow an interesting aspect that is revealed. Or because your initial plan isn't yielding anything worthwhile. Or you are meeting resistance and finding that something is too sensitive. Your research questions will be likely to change and develop as well. See Cresswell (2003) which will help you get a feel for the range of research traditions using this kind of approach. Of the approaches considered in this chapter, action research, case studies, ethnographic and feminist research, grounded theory studies and qualitative research almost always call for a flexible design, as do many documentary analyses and several types of evaluation research.

Flexible designs almost always rely heavily on collecting qualitative data. Fixed designs almost always rely heavily on collecting quantitative data. Indeed they have in the past been commonly referred to as qualitative and quantitative designs respectively. However, in principle, there is nothing to stop the use of methods yielding qualitative data in fixed designs, or ones yielding quantitative data in flexible designs – there can be considerable advantage in using a mixture of methods in many situations.

The demands on the researcher are rather different in the two approaches. Some would find it very difficult to cope with the uncertainties, and need to re-evaluate one's position and possibly make major changes, central to flexible design research. Others will find this an exhilarating challenge. Some would welcome the security and satisfaction of rolling out a well thought through detailed plan. Others want to get their hands dirty early on, and find the need for extensive pre-planning off-putting.

It is as well to know where you stand on these issues before committing yourself. However, as discussed in the next chapter, p. 51, fixed and flexible designs are best fitted to rather different types of research question. So, in effect, there will be constraints on the questions you can target, if you don't feel comfortable with the particular demands of one of the styles.

Overview of Some Different Research Traditions

The approaches listed below are just some of the different styles that have been used in research involving people. The advantage of working within an established research tradition is that many of the problems and pitfalls have already been thought through. The fact that there are agreed ways of doing things gives reassurance. However, it does mean that you need at least a basic knowledge of what is involved if you are planning to use one of these approaches. This will call for additional reading, or assistance from someone with relevant experience.

Don't think of the approaches as being totally separate or mutually exclusive. With ingenuity you could probably devise projects combining any two (even three or more) of the approaches covered here

If you are brave (foolhardy?) you may want to strike out on your own and not follow the well-trodden path. In practice, whatever you do is almost inevitably going to have features of one or more existing research traditions. So you may as well capitalize on the experience of others. They are presented in alphabetical order to try to avoid giving the impression that some approaches are superior to others.

Action research

An approach that emphasizes the involvement of the researcher in a situation or practice, with a view to improving it. The focus can be virtually anything, but is typically some kind of organization such as a support service (e.g. the advice service provided by a student union in a college). A central feature is the direct participation in the research of the people the research focuses on (e.g. the advisers and the users of the support service).

It is not an easy option by any means, but can be very rewarding – particularly if you can show that there is the improvement you hoped for. But beware, much social research of this kind has depressingly meagre positive outcomes.

You will need good social and organizational skills to bring off an action research project successfully. It will probably call for negotiation with individuals and groups of different kinds who have some kind of stake in what you are proposing (the stakeholders). They can range from the (probably high status) persons who have to agree to your being involved, through possibly apprehensive or hostile workers in the organization, to users or clients who will have their own concerns. Action research is an approach that can often, with benefit, be carried out on a group basis. Hopefully, different members of the group will have, between them, a range of appropriate skills.

There are many variants of action research, but it is seen typically as a cyclical process. In a simple form, this involves:

☐ planning a change of some kind (after discussion and consultation with all involved – not just at the whim of the researcher)
☐ finding out what happens after the change
☐ reflecting on this (again not just you, but in collaboration)
☐ planning further action.

The whole cycle can then be repeated, but in a small project, the first cycle is likely to be as much as you can get through. The cyclical nature of the research process, where later steps are dependent on the outcome of earlier ones, precludes a detailed pre-specification of the design and hence action research is typically flexible in design. Box 2.1 shows some of the advantages and disadvantages of the action research approach.

Action research can use a wide variety of data collection methods, depending on the type of research question to which you seek answers. Much action research relies heavily on qualitative data, usually in the form of words, obtained from relatively unstructured interviews or participant observation. However, collection of quantitative data from structured interviews or structured observation is by no means ruled out (see chapter 4 for details of the various methods).

Action research is commonly trying to establish the value of what is happening in an organization, perhaps focusing on a proposed new way of working or delivering a service. As such it is a particular way of carrying out an evaluation – see below p. 32. Much action research relies mainly on methods that produce qualitative data. Note, however, that there is nothing to rule out the use of

Box *2.1* Advantages and disadvantages of the action research approach

Advantages

1 A collaborative approach gives an active role to participants, hence a more democratic form of research than most approaches.
2 It is particularly suitable for practitioner-researchers, contributing to their professional and personal development.
3 The effect that the presence of the researcher has on the situation is integral to action research rather than a methodological problem.
4 It provides a means of addressing and resolving practical problems.
5 If successful, it can institute a continuing cycle of development and change in an organization.

Disadvantages

1 The involved collaborative stance required is difficult for a novice researcher.
2 Access can be difficult for all apart from 'insider' researchers.
3 The shared ownership of the research process between researcher and participant can lead to problems, particularly in completion of the project on time.
4 Active co-operation by participants is essential, but is difficult to achieve as it takes place in the work setting where there can be conflicting demands.
5 The non-traditional researcher role called for, with its inevitable loss in detachment and impartiality, may not be acceptable in some course regulations.

quantitative methods – perhaps by including a survey – see below p. 41. Such inter-relationships between different approaches, or traditions of research, are a common feature.

Further reading

Coghlan, B. and Brannick, T. (2004) *Doing Action Research in Your Own Organisation*. 2nd edition. London and Thousand Oaks, CA: Sage. Easy to follow. Gives both basics of action research and practical details of how to carry one out in your own organization.

Costello, P. (2003) *Action Research*. London and New York: Continuum. Focuses on practitioner research.

McNiff, J., Lomax, P. and Whitehead, J. (2003) *You and Your Action Research Project*. 2nd edition. London: Routledge Falmer. Strong on practicalities.

Case studies

As the name indicates, a case study is the study of a case. The case can be virtually anything. At one extreme the case might be an individual person, perhaps, in an educational context, a child. With a wider focus, the case might be a ward in a hospital or an office in a business. Wider still, the case could be an organization such as a golf club or a school. At the other extreme, it could be a global event such as the tsunami in the Indian ocean in December 2004, or famine in a developing country.

Cases are selected because they are, in some way, interesting or important. A 'failing' school; a bullying child; a successful entrepreneur; a house-husband; or the new thermal baths in the city of Bath where I live (at the time of writing, several years late in opening and vastly over-budget).

The case is studied in its own right. The prime concern is to find out something about that specific child, organization, or whatever. A good case study does throw light on wider issues, but this is often mainly because the reader of a case study report is able to draw parallels, or see similarities, with other situations and with their own concerns.

Cases are studied in their context. Some research traditions such as experiments and surveys effectively strip away the context of the phenomenon of interest as complicating the issue and compromising the degree of control seen as necessary. However an understanding of its setting is crucial to understanding why the case is as it is.

Case studies suffer by being viewed by some as a soft option. The choice that a weaker or lazier student might make. If this were ever true, it is not so now. To count as research, they have to be done to demanding standards. Robert Yin, who has had a major role in rescuing case study as a serious research strategy, emphasizes the need to use multiple sources of evidence (see the texts by Yin in the further reading list below). For example, interviews might be combined with observation, and documents of various types could be collected and analysed.

This is, in part, because we need to find ways of reassuring ourselves and readers that what we claim are the findings of a case study are trustworthy; literally, worthy of trust. There is a variety of things that can be done to this end (see chapter 4, p. 71). One of these, particularly important with case studies, is the collection of data using two or more different methods. If the different methods point to the same conclusion, this gives a better 'fix' on the phenomenon of interest (this is analogous to the approach used in surveying to establish position, known as *triangulation*, and is sometimes referred to as 'method triangulation'). There is, of course, the possibility that the different methods do not agree, which means that you will have to dig deeper to try to come up with the reasons for this. Doing this may give you a headache, but can possibly lead to unexpected insights.

Because case studies focus on a particular 'thing' of some kind, at a particular point in time, and because all research must focus on something and take place at a specific time, it follows that all research is in some sense a case study. Viewing your research project in this light can be of advantage. It encourages you not only to have a serious concern for the person(s) or situations you are researching in their own right (not just as a 'sample' from some population as in a survey or experiment), but also to see it or them as necessarily in some context, whose effects need to be considered. And it encourages the use of multiple data collection methods.

Case studies have used a wide variety of data collection methods, with perhaps interviews and observation, both participant and non-participant, being the most common. It is also the style of research most likely to use more than one data collection method in the same study. Case study design is almost inevitably *flexible* rather than fixed, as it is very difficult to pre-specify in any detail exactly the 'who, what and where' of data collection. Box 2.2 shows some of the advantages and disadvantages of the case study approach.

Case studies can also be evaluations and be operated as action research. They can use one of the qualitative research approaches and/or be largely based on documentary analysis.

They are sometimes based on purely documentary sources. In such situations, it is highly desirable to have a range of documents of different types for analysis. However, the more usual role of documentary analysis in case studies is to act as a secondary approach.

Box *2.2* Advantages and disadvantages of the case study approach

Advantages

1 Studying a single case (or a small number of cases) gives the opportunity to carry out a study in depth, which can capture complexities, relationships and processes.
2 It strongly encourages the use of multiple methods of collecting data, and of multiple data sources.
3 The boundaries of the study (e.g. the amount of time involved and context covered) are flexible, and can often be tailored to the time and resources you have available.
4 It is less artificial and detached than traditional approaches such as experiments and surveys.
5 It can be used for a wide variety of research purposes and for widely different types of cases.

Disadvantages

1 The credibility of generalizations from case studies is often challenged. It depends on a different logic from that familiar in surveys.
2 Case studies typically seek to focus on situations as they occur naturally and hence observer effects caused by the presence of the researcher can be problematic.
3 The flexible nature of case study design means that you have to be prepared to modify your approach, depending on the results of your involvement. It can become difficult to keep to deadlines.
4 The continuing, though erroneous, view that case study is necessarily a 'soft option', may lead to it not being acceptable in some course regulations.

Further reading

Yin, R. K. (2002) *Case Study Research: Design and methods.* 3rd edition. London and Thousand Oaks, CA: Sage. The key text on case study design.

Yin, R. K. (2002) *Applications of Case Study Research.* 2nd edition. London and Thousand Oaks, CA: Sage. Gives a variety of applications in widely differing fields.

Yin, R. K. (2004) *The Case Study Anthology.* London and Thousand Oaks, CA: Sage. Detailed descriptions of different types of case study in different fields.

Documentary analysis

The term 'document' suggests a printed source of some kind. In research it is usually defined more widely to include photographs, films and other non-written sources. A research project can be based solely on the analysis of documentary evidence of one form or another (e.g. in historical or literature research). Typical printed or written documents include:

☐ minutes of meetings of various kinds
☐ formal and informal records of different bodies
☐ letters and diaries
☐ inspection and other reports, and
☐ electronic documents such as websites.

In case studies, and other approaches where documentary analysis is not the main mode, it is often a valuable supplement.

The distinctive feature of a document is that it can, and often does, exist totally independent of your research. That is, it has been produced for some other purpose. Documents of this kind are sometimes referred to as inadvertent sources, to distinguish them from the kind of documentary sources such as books, monographs, journal articles, etc., produced essentially for the purposes of research. The main advantage of documents is that your carrying out an analysis of the document has no effect on the document itself. Such possible effects, referred to as *reactivity*, bedevil much research. There is the logical problem that if your research affects the thing researched, you don't know what the situation is in the absence of the research.

The main disadvantage of using documents is that they have been produced for some other purpose; this will almost certainly affect their nature and content. Documents produced in advance of a school's inspection, or a college's submission for assessment of the quality of its courses, are going to paint the best possible picture. Historians have been much exercised by the problems of evaluating documentary evidence (see, for example Barzun and Graff, 2000).

There are two distinct approaches to documentary analysis. In one, the starting point is the selection of one or more key documents. By studying these sources, you begin to appreciate what kinds of things might be said about them, and hence develop your research questions. This leads to a search for answers, further study and analysis, refinement and probable reformulation of the questions, etc.

The alternative approach is to start from the research question or problem. From your previous reading you home onto a possible focus for your research and then develop a set of research questions. Hence it is closer to the pre-specified fixed design. The search is then for a set of documents that will provide you with the material to get some answers. In practice, these two apparently very different strategies may blend. The source-led researcher probably has in mind some questions that influence the selection of appropriate sources. The question-led researcher may well find the study of the selected sources changes the focus and the questions that seem important – or for which answers might be forthcoming from analysis of the documents.

The approach taken in the analysis of inadvertent documents is essentially the same as that called for when dealing with any source of information, as discussed in the following chapter, p. 54. However, because they have been produced for some non-research purpose, you have to be sensitive to the possible biases that the original purpose might have caused.

Knowing the intended audience for the document gives insights into likely bias. The more you can find out about the context in which the document was produced, and of the characteristics of its writer, the better. The basic rule is never to accept what the document says at face value, but to try to get at why it says what it does.

A central decision has to be made about the trustworthiness of the document. The language often gives unwitting (i.e. unintended by the author) evidence about how far it can be trusted. Emotive terms and polemic, rather than reasoned conclusions and apparently objective analysis, should raise your suspicions. While this may reduce the document's value as a truthful account, it can sometimes be of great value, giving clues as to a person's or group's real views about the topic at issue.

Documentary analysis may be the only style open to researchers in some fields where, perhaps because the focus is on past events, there is no possibility of direct access. It would be a preferred choice of research style for the introverted researcher. Interaction is with the text rather than with often troublesome people.

Note: Documentary analysis can be viewed, as here, as an overall approach to doing a research project, or more as a method of data collection which is useful in a range of different approaches (see chapter 4, p. 88). Box 4.6 lists its advantages and disadvantages). Further reading is also provided there.

Ethnographic research

Originating in social anthropology, this is an approach that seeks to understand the life and customs of people living in a particular culture. Anthropologists carried out these studies by close involvement, often of several years, in primitive or exotic cultures.

Ethnography is now frequently used in a range of social science disciplines and in related applied fields. It has commonly shrunk in scale from the anthropologist's 'full ethnography' covering many aspects of the culture, to a shorter, more focused study sometimes called a 'mini-ethnography' or an 'ethnographic-style' study, where the involvement is of the order of weeks rather than years. The focus has also typically changed from a tribe in New Guinea, to an aspect of the researcher's own society, such as a call centre, lap-dancing club, or hospital intensive-care ward (to name three widely varying locations).

Central to ethnographic approaches is the use of participant observation. This is a data collection technique (see chapter 4, p. 84) where the researcher is closely involved in the setting concerned, and has a negotiated and understood role within the culture. The role might be of a full member which, while potentially offering the greatest insights into the 'ways of the tribe', increases the possibility of 'going native' (i.e. losing any researcher detachment and only seeing things from an insider perspective). Also, if the group is infiltrated without the researcher revealing their research role, this raises severe ethical problems. Such 'covert' tactics might be considered ethical in some circumstances (say, in studying an extremist or illegal group where there could be societal benefit in understanding how it functions, but where revealing the research role would totally preclude the possibility of involvement). This kind of 'high risk' (not least to you the researcher) topic should be out of bounds to the novice. And hence it can be taken as axiomatic that your role as researcher should be declared and understood, whatever additional role you have within the group.

Participant observation typically leads to qualitative accounts in the form of notes and diaries. A practical difficulty is in getting a record of events and situations while they are fresh in your mind – this may call for a retreat round a corner or into a convenient broom cupboard or empty room. A good rule is not to go to sleep before you have produced an account of the day's events. Observation can be supplemented by interviews, particularly to clarify things that have puzzled you, or that you don't understand, and to check out your tentative interpretations. Interviews are usually informal, where you take the opportunity to 'have a word' whenever possible.

The design of an ethnographic study is necessarily flexible. Typically, a particular setting is chosen because of the researcher's general interest in that kind of setting, although it can usefully be selected because you can see its potential for getting answers to more specific questions. The fact that you can get easy access to a setting (perhaps because of personal or family connections, say, that you are already a member of a church, orchestra, or whatever) is not a negligible factor. If you can't get in, you can't do the research.

Whatever research questions you start with, it is as well not to be too committed to them. It is highly likely that your involvement and observation will cause them to evolve. Or you might appreciate that you need to think about what is going on in a totally different way, throwing up a new set of research questions.

Box 2.3 lists some of the advantages and disadvantages of the ethnographic approach.

Flexibility is an inherent part of an ethnographic study. Some researchers revel in it. Others find it extremely stressful. You can prepare yourself in various ways for ethnographic style research (read, talk to people, sort out the practicalities including access and what role you will have), but you are not going to be able to have a plan of campaign that just unrolls as decided in advance.

Further reading

Brewer, J. D. (2000) *Ethnography*. Maidenhead, Berks: Open University Press. Discusses current controversies about ethnography, as well as providing guidelines for good practice.

Crang, M. and Cook, I. (2006) *Doing Ethnography*. London and Thousand Oaks, CA: Sage. Useful practical guide for the first-time ethnographer. Covers both issues and methods.

Silverman, D. (2004) *Doing Qualitative Research: A practical handbook*. 2nd edition. London and Thousand Oaks, CA: Sage. Covers ethnography together with

Box 2.3 Advantages and disadvantages of the ethnographic approach

Advantages

1 Ethnographic style studies (as distinct from so-called 'full ethnographies') are feasible within the constraints of time and resources of undergraduate projects.
2 They rely largely upon direct observation and do not call for other specialized data collection methods.
3 They are particularly suitable for studies focusing on how members of a culture see events.
4 They result in rich data focusing on processes and relationships set in context.
5 They can be very involving and interesting.

Disadvantages

1 They can be very difficult and confusing for the novice researcher to come to terms with their participant observer role (tensions between being a participant and an observer).
2 The skills needed to understand what is going on in a strange situation, including decisions on the choice of informants may need considerable experience to acquire. Practitioner-researchers working in familiar settings have the converse problem of 'making the familiar strange' (i.e. needing to set aside their preconceptions).
3 Ethnography traditionally seeks to move from the purely descriptive to provide theoretical explanations, which is not an easy task.
4 Ethical issues abound, including the avoidance of deception (e.g. about one's role), obtaining informed consent and intrusions on privacy.
5 Access can be difficult to obtain.
6 There are problems of generalizability of findings similar to those with case studies.

other qualitative approaches. Hands-on practical guide to all aspects of doing a qualitative project. Wide range of examples.

Evaluation research

Evaluation is, currently, flavour of the millennium in most, if not yet all, applied fields. To evaluate is to assess the worth or value of something. That 'something' can be as various as the case in case study, but is typically some innovation, intervention, service or organization. Evaluations don't always qualify as research.

They may not have the concern for truth discussed at the beginning of this chapter, but may be carried out for some other (possibly undeclared) motive. For example, an evaluation of a service or innovation that is stirring things up may be carried out with the covert intention to provide justification for closing it down. Or the evaluation of the effectiveness of a new diet might be funded by its promoters to boost sales.

Using the term 'evaluation research' here signals the avoidance of such dubious practices. The triple requirements of carrying out research systematically, sceptically, and, above all, ethically (p. 19) should be your watchwords.

Evaluation is much called for in both public service and private businesses because of current concerns for accountability and value for money. These are legitimate and understandable concerns. However, the results are not always benign. Apart from the questionable practices discussed above, problems can occur because of the insensitivity of evaluators. Evaluation is, almost inevitably, highly anxiety-making for those evaluated. Even when intentions are honourable, and there is a full and truthful account given of what is proposed, suspicions remain. Other problems derive from inappropriate assumptions about the nature and purpose of a particular evaluation. For example, in some circles it is assumed that an evaluation should be simply and solely concerned with assessing whether certain prescribed goals have been achieved. Admittedly this can be what is needed, but it is by no means the only possible type of evaluation.

As ever, the touchstone advocated in this text is – first sort out your research questions and then work out what you need to do to get answers. In evaluation research, different types of research question are linked to the different purposes one might have in carrying out an evaluation. Box 2.4 covers some of the possibilities. While questions 4 and 5 are in the same broad area, question 5 asks something wider than simply whether prescribed goals are reached. As many interventions involving people have unintended and unanticipated

---

Box 2.4 Some general evaluation questions

1 What is needed (in relation to something that is proposed)?
2 Does what is provided meet the needs of those involved?
3 What happens when it is in operation?
4 Does it attain its goals or objectives?
5 What are its outcomes?
6 How do costs and benefits compare?
7 Does it meet required standards?
8 Should it continue?
9 How can it be improved?

consequences this can be a very useful broadening – though it might be resisted by those afraid of your finding out something they didn't want to know.

The other questions take one into very different areas, each of which might be of legitimate concern. Note that there is nothing in itself wrong or unethical about carrying out research to establish whether it is appropriate for a particular service, programme, or intervention to continue (question 8). That is, provided it is made clear from the outset that this question is on the agenda, and that the question is being approached with an open mind and no pre-set agenda. Indeed, a team running the service or whatever, and convinced that it is fulfilling a useful function, could welcome the evaluation. However, this is one of the more sensitive types of evaluation and as a new researcher I would think twice (at least) before becoming involved.

Box 2.5 shows some of the advantages and disadvantages of the evaluation research approach. Evaluations can, and often do, focus on one particular setting or situation, i.e. they are also case studies. In fact, an evaluation could be conducted in such a way that it could also be viewed as an example of almost all the other approaches considered here. It could be purely qualitative, though evaluations often combine different data collection methods resulting in both qualitative and quantitative data. Evaluations have also made use of a wide variety of data collection methods.

Box 2.5 Advantages and disadvantages of the evaluation research approach

Advantages

1 It provides a research tool for addressing the accountability now called for in almost all areas of society.
2 There is a wide variety of types of evaluation suitable for many different research questions.
3 Sensitively handled, evaluations have an important role in improving services and the functioning of organizations.

Disadvantages

1 It should be approached with care by novice researchers owing to the almost inevitable sensitivity of an evaluative study.
2 Ethical issues abound, particularly concerning evaluations that may result in harm to any of those involved.
3 Access is problematic. Even when formal access is granted, there can be internal resistance and obstruction.

An evaluation could be carried out as a piece of action research. When the interest is on whether objectives have been met (or more generally, on what the outcomes are), an evaluation can be built around an experiment or survey. The randomized controlled trial (RCT), a form of experimental approach, is strongly advocated by those following currently popular 'evidence-based' approaches. Many evaluations make use of some kind of documentary analysis, though this would usually be only a part of the research. The usual principle applies – the design of an evaluation is determined by the research questions you want to answer – and hence by the purposes of the evaluation.

An evaluation research project can be either fixed or flexible in design depending on the specific approach taken.

Further reading

Hall, I. and Hall, D. (2004) *Evaluation and Social Research: Introducing small-scale practice*. Basingstoke: Palgrave Macmillan. Very practical and down to earth, with extensive real-life examples.

Robson, C. (2000) *Small-scale Evaluation: Principles and practice*. London and Thousand Oaks, CA: Sage. Covers a wide range of types of evaluation from the perspective of practitioner-researchers, and of those new to evaluation.

Weiss, C. H. (1997) *Evaluation: Methods for studying programs and policies*. 2nd edition. Upper Saddle River, NJ: Prentice Hall. Integrates a theory-based approach with practical guidance on all aspects of carrying out an evaluation.

Experiments

To experiment can simply mean to try out something new or different. In research, however, it usually means something much more specific. There are arguments about exactly what is entailed, but these features are typical:

☐ selection of a small number of variables* for investigation
☐ active manipulation or change of one or more of these variables by the experimenter
☐ measurement of the effect of this manipulation on one or more other variables, and
☐ control of a range of other variables.

An experiment is a very precise tool that should only be used when there is a considerable amount known about the phenomenon studied. Without such

---

* A variable is a measure which can take on different values (e.g. heart rate, income, sex).

knowledge it is very difficult to decide exactly which variables are to be studied and how they should be measured. The active role of the experimenter, and the tight control of the situation needed to run a successful experiment, is controversial in some areas and difficult or even impossible to achieve in many fields of social research.

Nevertheless, experiments and their findings are typically highly valued. This is largely because they have been viewed as the best means of establishing causation. The argument, in simplified form, is that, if the change in a variable by the experimenter (in experiment-speak known as the independent variable) is accompanied by changes in another variable (called the dependent variable) when all other relevant variables are being held constant or otherwise controlled, then the change in the independent variable caused the change in the dependent variable.

A particular form of the experiment is claimed by its advocates as the 'gold standard' for research. This is the so-called 'true' experiment. Perhaps the simplest form of this is the randomized controlled trial or RCT. Here, the independent variable has two values; one is referred to as 'experimental', the other as 'control' (the former, perhaps, a new drug; the control, a placebo of sugar pills). Participants in the trial are then randomly assigned to the experimental or control groups. The randomization provides a means of controlling for other variables associated with those taking part in the experiment (e.g. gender, background, general health status). The argument goes that, while these variables might well affect performances on the dependent variable, random assignment means that they are as likely to be associated with higher performance as with lower. Of course, in any particular study, chance factors might affect the result but the use of statistical theory can assess the probability that a difference in performance between experimental and control groups is due to such chance factors. And, if this probability is sufficiently low (often, conventionally, set at 5 per cent), then the argument goes that, if the difference is unlikely to be due to chance, then it can reasonably be concluded that the effect on the dependent variable was caused by the change in the independent variable – i.e. in this case the effect of the new drug.

It is clear that, in many fields of research, experiments are here to stay. They can provide quantitative evidence that convinces several audiences including government and other policy-makers. However, they are no panacea. As indicated above, they can only be carried out with a realistic chance of success in well understood fields. An experiment is not a tool for exploration of a new area. A result of an experiment by itself gives little help in explaining why that result has been obtained.

Experiments are best carried out in laboratory settings, which are effectively environments designed to maximize control over extraneous variables. Outside the laboratory the necessary control is hard to achieve. There may well be ethical as well as practical concerns, both about the control needed to set up the experiment, and the active role of the experimenter, who is changing something which may be important in people's lives. At a more specific level, there can be both practical difficulties and ethical objections to the random assignment of participants, which is the hallmark of the true experiments. This has led to the development of so-called quasi-experimental designs, which follow the same basic experimental approach but without random assignment. For example, in educational settings it may only be possible to work with existing classes of pupils rather than randomly assigning them to different experimental conditions. So, we might use two or more parallel classes from a particular year group. With careful design it is possible to eliminate many possible alternative explanations of differences found between the classes and be confident that these differences are attributable to the experimental treatment.

Experimental designs are many and varied. If you are inexperienced, it is wise to stick to simple designs, though you need not be restricted to the very simplest where only a single independent variable is manipulated, and where that variable has only two levels (e.g. experimental and control conditions). You could go for, say, a couple of variables with one of them having three or more levels (perhaps comparing two or three different experimental conditions with a control).

Useful quasi-experimental designs include ones where for practical or ethical reasons you have to work with intact groups rather than being able to use random allocation to assign participants to groups as discussed above. An alternative approach is to use a time-series design, where a sequence of equivalent measures on a dependent variable are made before and after some intervention or change. The interpretation of the results of quasi-experimental designs is more problematic than those from true designs. There are some commonly used designs (e.g. where comparisons are made between the performance of two non-randomly assigned groups after an intervention) which should be avoided, because they do not provide convincing evidence that differences between the performance of the groups is attributable to the intervention. There are alternative explanations of the differences that it is impossible to discount (e.g. that it is due to pre-existing differences between the groups).

A radically different approach to traditional experimental design is known as single-case (sometimes referred to as single-subject) design. This also makes use of sequences of measurements or observations made over a period of time, but it differs from traditional time-series designs by focusing on individuals rather than groups. It is often associated with the controversial psychologist B. F. Skinner, who developed a range of such designs. While the simplest single-case designs share the interpretation difficulties of simple quasi-experimental designs, there are more complex alternatives, such as multiple base-line designs, which are more adequate (see, for example, the text by Richards et al. 1999 in the further reading below).

Box 2.6 shows some of the advantages and disadvantages of the experimental approach. Experiments stand alone as a very particular way of carrying out research. They are the epitome of fixed design research. As indicated above, they can be used in certain types of evaluation, usually those focusing on outcomes. This apart, they do not sit happily with the other approaches considered here. They employ data collection methods that produce the kind of quantitative data amenable to statistical analysis. Some form of test or scale, or structured observation instrument is commonly used, the actual method being especially devised for each experiment. A secondary data collection method, such as having a short interview with participants after their experimental involvement to probe their perception of the experience, can often be useful.

Box 2.6 Advantages and disadvantages of the experimental approach

Advantages

1 It provides the possibility of getting clear and unambiguous answers to very specific research questions.
2 The very tight specification of the conditions of the laboratory experiment permits replication and hence the checking of findings.
3 Laboratory experiments eliminate the problem of gaining access. You don't have to spend time and resources travelling to and from the site of the research.
4 It is regarded traditionally as the method of choice for demonstrating causal relationships.

Disadvantages

1 It is not feasible unless there is extensive prior knowledge about the topic.
2 It is difficult to avoid artificiality, particularly in laboratory experiments, making the application of findings to real world issues problematic.
3 The control by the experimenter of relevant variables central to experimentation can raise difficult ethical problems.
4 This control can be difficult to achieve in field experiments.
5 Finding a statistically significant result does not, in itself, help to explain why the result was obtained.

Further reading

Barlow, D. H. and Hersen, M. (2006) *Single Case Experimental Designs*. 3rd edition. Upper Saddle River, NJ: Allyn and Bacon. Big reference text covering a wide range of single case designs. Second edition still useful.

Field, A. and Hole, G. J. (2002) *How to Design and Report Experiments*. London and Thousand Oaks, CA: Sage. Lucid, accessible and pretty comprehensive. Welcome emphasis on design.

Maxwell, S. E. and Delaney, H. D. (2003) *Designing Experiments and Analyzing Data: A model comparison perspective*. Mahwah, NJ: Lawrence Erlbaum Associates. Comprehensive reference text. The model comparison approach has much to commend it over traditional approaches. Some statistics background needed.

Richards, S. B., Taylor, R. L., Ramasamy, R. and Richards, R. Y. (1999) *Single Subject Research and Design: Applications in Educational and Clinical Settings*. London: Singular Press. Concise and clear guidance on carrying out a range of single-subject designs.

Robson, C. (1994) *Experiment, Design and Statistics in Psychology*. 3rd edition. Harmondsworth: Penguin. Simple introduction. Full text available without charge from author's Blackwell website (www.blackwellpublishing.com/robson/ebook.htm).

Grounded theory studies

The grounded theory approach arose within sociology as a reaction to the previous 'grand theory' approach where, essentially, the task of research was to provide validation for (or disconfirmation of) theoretical formulations. Grounded theory, associated with the work of Barney Glaser and Anselm Strauss, takes the opposite tack. Their view was that theory should arise from, be 'grounded' in, empirical research; i.e. from the findings of actual research studies. Their text *The Discovery of Grounded Theory* (Glaser and Strauss, 1967) has stimulated a host of studies, not only in sociology but also in many other social science disciplines and in related applied fields. There are, however more accessible later texts, including Strauss and Corbin (1998).

As with several other approaches to research arising largely from the pronouncements of specific individuals, there are essentially two ways of doing a grounded theory study. Either one sticks closely to the procedures advocated by the originators or one follows their general ideas.

The former strategy is complicated by the fact that Glaser and Strauss have subsequently diverged somewhat in their views about how grounded theory studies should be conducted. Whichever version of the gospel is followed there is a specific and detailed set of procedures that some will find attractive. All the more so because, as with ethnographic style studies, there is an inherent flexibility in the quest. The themes, the ways in which the data are to be best understood, are considered to emerge from the data rather than being pre-ordained and imposed. The procedure, in the popular Strauss and Corbin version, involves a three-stage coding process discussed in chapter 6, p. 132, in the context of analysing qualitative data.

For those, including myself, who rather take exception to the requirement that analysis of the data must be done in particular ways, and find difficulty in the assertion that it is possible to approach any research without having some presuppositions arising from prior experience or reading, a study following their general approach is perhaps more attractive. A large proportion of flexible design projects can be approached in this way. All that is called for is a relatively open-ended starting point, where any initial research questions (from your reading or experience) are seen as tentative and subject to modification as the project develops. You start with data analysis, using the process discussed in chapter 6, at an early stage in the data collection process, and then use the results of this ongoing coding to help shape later data collection. When data collection is finished, further analysis clarifies the questions to which you now have answers. Put in other terms, you are seeking to develop a theory of how you can best understand what is going on, grounded in the data.

Box 2.7 shows some of the advantages and disadvantages of the grounded theory approach.

Box *2.7* Advantages and disadvantages of the grounded theory approach

Advantages

1 It is widely used as a method for generating or deriving theory from a research project (usually, but not necessarily, qualitative).
2 It provides useful prescriptions for the process of carrying out flexible design projects.
3 It provides a detailed set of rules and procedures for the coding and analysis of qualitative data.

Disadvantages

1 The very specific terminology and highly prescriptive coding rules have acquired something of a cult status (however it is possible to adopt the general style of the approach without buying in to all of this).
2 Strict insistence that the theory must be generated from the data collected ignores what researchers bring to the analysis from their previous experience and reading.
3 There are different variants of grounded theory now put forward by its founders.

Further reading

Charmaz, K. C. (2005) *Grounded Theory for the 21st Century*. London and Thousand Oaks, CA: Sage. Practical introduction with good range of worked examples. Doesn't follow the Glaser and Strauss line closely.

Silverman, D. (2004) *Doing Qualitative Research: A practical handbook*. 2nd edition. London and Thousand Oaks, CA: Sage. Covering grounded theory, together with other qualitative approaches. Hands-on practical guide to all aspects of doing a qualitative project. Wide range of examples.

Strauss, A. and Corbin, J. (1998) *Basics of Qualitative Research: Techniques and procedures for developing grounded theory*. 2nd edition. London and Thousand Oaks, CA: Sage. A practical introduction to doing a qualitative project based on grounded theory.

Surveys

Of the various possible approaches to research, the survey is possibly the simplest to carry out. This may account, in part, for its popularity. Its findings also communicate well to different audiences, including the general public. However, while it is easy to carry out a survey, it is much more difficult to carry out a good one.

A survey typically involves seeking answers to a number of standard questions from a carefully selected group of people. A questionnaire is devised and is either given, or sent out, to people for self-completion or administered face-to-face in an interview situation (or, increasingly, via the telephone). Other surveys rely purely on observation, as in surveys of traffic, or the use of some facility such as a library.

Central to most surveys is the notion that the persons questioned, or events observed, are a sample of a wider population. In a good survey, the sample selected is representative of the population. If this is the case, what we find from the sample gives us unbiased information about the population as a whole. Perhaps we are interested in the attitudes of teenagers to some issue of current interest – say whether the age for voting in national elections should be reduced. The population of interest might be all teenagers in the country. Or it might be more specific, say, 16-year-olds in a particular political constituency, or a school or college. Assuming that you can't question all members of the target population (if you can, as in a school or college population then fine – technically this is known as a *census* rather than a survey), then you need to have a scheme for selecting the sample. The sampling issue crops up frequently in research and is returned to in chapter 5, p. 97.

Many surveys suffer from poor response rates. The phenomenon of questionnaire-fatigue is increasingly common with some target groups ('Not another ***** questionnaire!'). This is a predictable response to situations where they feel that they are being, or have been, used for the researchers' benefit, and has to be taken seriously. The problem with poor response rates is that, as explained above, a central rationale for the survey is to generalize from sample to population. This differs crucially from the case study approach, where the intention is to try to find out things about the actual case, or cases, studied, in their own right. With a low survey response rate, generalization of findings to the population can't be done with any confidence. Logically, we do not know the way in which those who did not respond would have responded if they did. It may well be that the non-responders have different views and characteristics to those who do respond. The solution is to use every effort to secure high responses in the first place. Incidentally, it is not feasible to give hard and fast rules about what constitutes an acceptably high response rate, but anything below the 70 per cent rate is a cause for serious concern. It has to be admitted though that studies with low response rates continue to be published in journals.

Survey design is not as complex a subject as experimental design, but shouldn't be ignored. A poor survey consists of a set of questions just dreamed up because they seemed to be of interest or of relevance. A good survey is one with demonstrable links between survey questions and research questions, and well crafted survey questions. It is very unlikely that you will be able to ask your research questions directly, but you have to ask the questionnaire questions in such a way that the answers are relevant to the research questions.

There is also considerable expertise needed to work out the best way of framing the questions. Much of this is obvious (don't ask long and complicated questions; don't ask leading questions – i.e. ones which push toward particular answers, etc.).

Overall, the survey is a deservedly popular approach to research. It is not difficult to design, carry out or report on. However, it's by no means an easy option. A good worthwhile survey calls for considerable attention to detail and persistence. The survey is, together with the experiment, one of the prime examples of fixed design research. Box 2.8 shows some of the advantages and disadvantages of the survey approach.

Surveys are rarely combined with other approaches, though some combinations are feasible (e.g. with action research or an evaluation). Methods producing quantitative data (or where responses can be turned into such data) are almost always used. Questionnaires, either used in interview situations or for self-completion, are most often used. There are other possibilities including the use of structured observation.

Note: As noted when discussing documentary analysis, a survey can be viewed as an overall approach to doing a research project, or more as a method of data collection which is useful in a range of different approaches.

Box 2.8 Advantages and disadvantages of the survey approach

Advantages

1 It is a very widely used approach whose results communicate well with many different audiences.
2 It typically produces quantitative data that can be easily subjected to statistical analysis, using straightforward computer-based techniques.
3 It is a fixed design approach where it is possible to predict relatively accurately the amount of time and resources needed to complete data collection and analysis.
4 Large sample sizes can be sought without major cost implications (a major proportion of the cost is associated with design of the questionnaire).
5 Use of representative samples from known populations leads to readily generalizable results where the situation in the population can be estimated with known probability.

Disadvantages

1 There can be misplaced confidence in the findings, particularly when there are deficiencies in sampling or response rates are relatively low.
2 It is increasingly difficult to achieve acceptable response rates from the widely used postal survey.
3 Checking on the seriousness or honesty with which respondents approach the task of completing a survey is difficult.
4 Surveys usually lack detail and depth as lengthy and complex questionnaires will affect response rates.
5 Surveys do not permit exploration of the context of the phenomenon studied.

Further reading

Aldridge, A. and Levine, K. (2001) Surveying the Social World: Principles and practice in social research. Maidenhead, Berks: Open University Press. Practical text giving useful advice to those with limited resources.

Czaja, R. and Blair, J. (2004) Designing Surveys: A guide to decisions and procedures. 2nd edition. Thousand Oaks, CA: Pine Forge. Comprehensive coverage. All you need to design and run a professional standard survey.

Lavrakas, P. J. (1993) Telephone Survey Methods: Sampling, selection and supervision. London and Thousand Oaks, CA: Sage. Detailed coverage of telephone surveys.

A note on feminist research

Feminist research is sometimes viewed as a particular and distinctive approach to research. Certainly researchers working under this banner have made a substantial contribution to research methodology and to views of how research should be carried out. There is an emphasis, for example, on the need for an involved, rather than a detached, stance to the persons on whom the research focuses. The influence that the researcher's own values have on the process and outcomes of the research is acknowledged. Qualitative research is typically given a privileged position over quantitative research by feminist researchers, though there are counter-examples. However, while some have maintained that there is a distinctive set of research methods appropriate for feminist researchers, it seems that in practice no particular method is universally ruled in or ruled out.

Further reading

Hesse-Biber, S. N. and Yaiser, M., eds. (2003) *Feminist Perspectives on Social Research*. Oxford: Oxford University Press. Includes over 20 chapters on applications and methods covering a wide range of approaches from feminist perspectives.

Reinharz, S. and Davidman, L. (1992) *Feminist Methods in Social Research*. Oxford: Oxford University Press. Analyses the relationship between feminism and methodology. Wide-ranging and thoughtful discussion of the contribution made to research methods by feminist researchers.

Roberts, H., ed. (1981) *Doing Feminist Research*. London: Routledge. Interesting and influential set of chapters from a feminist perspective, raising practical, methodological, theoretical and ethical issues.

Choosing an Approach

The approaches discussed here by no means exhaust the existing approaches to research you might consider. There are, for example, a host of different styles of qualitative research each of which has passionate adherents. These include:

☐ *Hermeneutic research* An approach based upon the analysis and interpretation of texts. Originally developed from biblical scholarship and dealing with written texts, but more recently virtually anything (e.g. clothing, architecture) has been viewed as a kind of text. It is a particular form of documentary analysis (see above, p. 27)

☐ *Phenomenological research* This focuses on the subjective experience of the individuals studied and seeks to understand and describe what happens to them from their own point of view

☐ *Discourse analysis* This focuses on how language, both spoken and written, is used in social contexts. The main concern is to recognize the regularities in language – what patterns are there; what repertoires do participants have. It calls for very detailed analysis, usually of relatively small language samples.

☐ *Narrative analysis* This involves the collection of narratives or stories and is used in studying lives and lived experience. It avoids the decontextualization and fragmentation of accounts when split into coded segments (as in grounded theory).

See the website for material discussing each of these approaches.

Don't worry if you find the range of possible approaches somewhat overwhelming. My intention in introducing them has been to help break down any assumptions that research **must**, *or* **must not**, *be carried out in one particular way, as well as to get you thinking about what approach you might take in your project.*

Base your choice of approach on:

☐ Do you know enough about the approach to do a good job? (If not, can you find out, with available help, enough to cope in the time available?)
☐ Is it feasible in the time, and with the resources, you have available?
☐ Are you suited to the approach temperamentally (some people might find doing an experiment aversive, others might have the same reaction to participant observation; some like the security of a fixed design where you sort out details of procedures before collecting data, others prefer the challenge of responding to what you find and amending plans, typical of flexible designs)? And, crucially
☐ Will it provide answers to your research questions?

Chapter 3 concentrates on what you have to do to sort out a sensible set of research questions. The strategy at this stage is, therefore, to hold back until you are clear about these questions. Bear in mind, however, that a mismatch between approach and research question can be sorted out by changing either the approach, or the set of questions (or both).

Further Reading

Cresswell, J. W. (2003) *Research Design: Qualitative, quantitative and mixed method approaches.* 2nd edition. London and Thousand Oaks, CA: Sage. Deservedly popular. Wide ranging and accessible.

Hakim, C. (2000) *Research Design: Successful designs for social economic research.* 2nd edition. London: Routledge. Revised version of one of the first texts to deal systematically with all aspects of research design. Examples from a wide range of disciplines including applied research.

de Vaus, D. (2001) *Research Design in Social Research*. London and Thousand Oaks, CA: Sage. Stresses the crucial importance of design. Covers a range of different designs with a large number of examples.

See also the suggestions for further reading on specific approaches, provided after discussion of that approach.

Chapter 2 Tasks

1 Write into your project diary any ideas that have come to you as a result of reading this chapter (the same applies to the following chapters, so I won't keep repeating it). In particular, note any revisions to your original thoughts about what you might do and *first thoughts about how you might do it*, arising from reading this chapter.

Don't push this though if you aren't at all sure. The next chapter concentrates on getting your ideas into focus.

2 *Prepare for action* Before you get into the hurly-burly of doing the project, it is a good idea to get yourself sorted out on as many dimensions as possible. I like to think of a research project as a 'little life'. You are starting out with a clean slate (not really, but it helps to think that you are) and you have the opportunity of being well organized and prepared, on top of things, etc. For example:

☐ *Clear your deck/desk* Sorting out your personal circumstances so that you have the physical and mental space to put your best efforts into the project
☐ *Get your computer in good order* Make sure you have the software you need and know how to use it efficiently. In particular, set up arrangements to maintain back-ups of the word-processing and other files that arise from the project. Don't be one of those unfortunate people who have a hard disc crash when finishing the project report – and have to type it all in again.

3

Developing Your Ideas

Selecting a Topic

The selection of a general topic area tends either to be straightforward and quick, or problematic and likely to eat up a lot of valuable time – unless you are careful. It is easy if you are following up on something you have already been involved with, or if the topic is decided by someone else. The boss says, 'do this', or your supervisor says 'select one from this list'.

In other situations, you need to give topic selection careful thought. Keep your eyes and ears open. Talk to people – colleagues, fellow students and your supervisor. Read voraciously. Dip into recent issues of academic and professional journals, serious newspapers and magazines. Follow tentative ideas up on the internet using Google or a similar search engine (see the section on sources later in the chapter, p. 56).

The topic should fulfil three main criteria:

☐ *It interests you* Doing a piece of research can be a very rewarding experience. Many students consider it to be the most valuable and worthwhile part of their whole degree course. However, it can be frustrating. All sorts of things can go wrong and some will. Having a real interest in the topic can keep you going through the inevitable sticky patches.

☐ *It will meet course requirements* As a student on a degree or other course, your primary audience is whoever will assess your work. There will be formal requirements about what is expected. These will mainly affect the type of study and how it is to be written up, rather than its focus.

☐ *It will be feasible for you to deliver something worthwhile on the topic given the available time and resources* Keep away from 'big' topics such as world peace or global warming. Though if something big really interests you, it may be feasible to focus on a particular small facet which is manageable.

Beware highly sensitive topics. Lacking experience, you may be out of your depth and cause harm. For example, a study of an innovatory scheme for drug users, unless carefully handled, may stimulate opposition and cause its termination.

Advisers may also recommend that you keep away from currently 'hot' topics; i.e. ones where there is much current interest. However, if you can come up with something new and different that fulfils the criteria, and/or you have useful access, consider going for it. Even popular areas like these are rarely fully worked out. The main practical disadvantage is that you will need to get on top of a substantial amount of recently completed, perhaps not very accessible, research.

A fairly common situation is to come up with two possible 'runners' which you can't decide between. Then, when you find out more about the first topic, you begin to appreciate its problems, and so the second topic seems more attractive. And when you find out more about the second topic . . . and so on. Go for the one that interests you more.

Box 3.1 lists a varied set of topics mainly harvested from an hour's surfing on the internet. The last two are derived from Dunbar (2005), who provides a rich source of interesting topics, based on case studies in the evaluation of research designs. While these topics vary tremendously in breadth, they all need substantial further focusing. The next step is to find out more about the topic. With some, there will be an embarrassment of riches – try a Google search on 'Homeless youth'. Here the problem is to see the wood for the trees, but there are usually fairly obvious pointers toward possible facets of the topic that might be more manageable. Perhaps the needs of pre-school homeless, or the effectiveness of compensatory education programmes for homeless school-age children. Similarly, 'Binge drinking' is, at the time of writing, an

---

Box 3.1 Examples of broad topic areas

Pets in sheltered housing for the elderly
Overcoming computer anxiety
Children and dinosaurs
Nanny care and language development
Homeless youth
Driving while talking on a mobile phone
Influence of TV lifestyle programmes
Educating children with behaviour problems in regular classes
Binge drinking
Graphology and job selection
Effects of video gaming

---

extremely 'hot' topic, particularly in the context of late night and early hours anti-social behaviour by young drinkers. Changing the focus to excessive drinking at home by senior citizens might be profitable.

A search on other topics – 'children and dinosaurs' for example, may throw up few leads. You may find this more attractive; moving into relatively uncharted waters.

Practitioner researchers can be highly constrained in the choice of a topic. It should not only be something that you consider both feasible and interesting, but also must meet with approval and support within your organization (both formally by management and more informally by colleagues – see the sections on access and 'insider research', chapter 5, p. 100).

Many topics can yield a worthwhile and feasible project with sufficient ingenuity and focusing. But there are topics you should steer clear of – Box 3.2 gives examples.

Box 3.2 Research topics to avoid

1 *Too big* Topics that demand more resources to complete in the time that you have available. Can be rescued by focusing on one aspect only.

2 *Too trivial* New researchers, frightened by warnings about limited resources, can go to the opposite extreme. Small can be beautiful. Some high quality projects research a single unit such as a classroom, but there has to be compensating depth and detail. Avoid the trivial. A very specific topic should be defensible as having some kind of wider relevance, to practice, theory, or whatever.

3 *Too difficult* Just because you can isolate an interesting topic, doesn't mean you can say anything worthwhile about it. There are often good reasons why a topic hasn't been previously researched.

4 *Too boring* Avoid a topic that doesn't interest you. Even if you complete it (and you might find it difficult to maintain motivation), others are also likely to find it boring.

5 *Ethically dubious* Steer clear of topics that you can't do without breaching ethical guidelines (e.g. putting participants at risk of harm or where findings might be used to harm or disadvantage someone). See the later section in this chapter, p. 64.

Replication research

A replication of a piece of research is an attempt to repeat it. In social research there is much concern about the replicability of findings from previous research; i.e. whether repeating the research would result in the same findings. A distinction is made between exact replications, which, as the term suggests, seek to repeat the study exactly, and constructive replications in which the original study is modified in one or more respects.

If you are interested in the findings of a piece of research you have come across, or if the findings seem suspect, there is much to be said for attempting a constructive replication of it. Not an exact replication though, as it might be argued that there is not enough of you in the exercise. Also your study probably couldn't be an exact replication anyway, as it necessarily takes place at a different time from the original and is probably in a context which differs in other important aspects. Check that a study of this type is acceptable in your course regulations.

From a Topic to Research Questions

Your first task is to move from the broad topic area to a more focused topic. Think of this as your working title for the project. It is often helpful to have a two part title, e.g. 'Why do children like dinosaurs? An exploratory study at a nursery school'. Or '"I couldn't take my cat": a study of policies in residential homes for the elderly, and their effects'. One part indicates the topic area. The other tells you something about the focus.

The second crucial and difficult task is to formulate the research questions to which your project will try to get answers. Resist the temptation to go out and collect data until you have at least a tentative set of possible questions.

In coming to a decision to go for a topic, and from the reading and discussions you have had along the way, you will probably already have an initial set of questions that you can write down. They are likely to be of different types. Some may be nuts-and-bolts questions of the 'who/what/where/when' kind (some 'why' ones wouldn't come amiss, either). Make a list of any and all questions you can come up with. Splurge – don't censor them for whether or not they are sensible. Box 3.3 gives an example.

This set of 20 questions is typical of most 'splurged' lists in being something of a mess. There are many more questions than one could hope to deal with adequately in a small-scale project; it is very teacher-oriented, and there is considerable overlap between several of the questions. Nevertheless, it is a useful starting point.

Box 3.3 An initial (unedited) set of research questions

1 How do teachers in secondary schools use interactive whiteboards?
2 What training have teachers had in the use of interactive whiteboards?
3 Which teaching subjects are interactive whiteboards most useful for?
4 Which pupil ages are interactive whiteboards most useful for?
5 Which ability groups are interactive whiteboards most useful for?
6 Does the use of interactive whiteboards by teachers vary with the age and experience of the teacher?
7 What do teachers consider to be the advantages of interactive whiteboards?
8 What do teachers consider to be the disadvantages of interactive whiteboards?
9 What factors affect the extent to which teachers use interactive whiteboards?
10 What are the difficulties in using interactive whiteboards?
11 Why are some teachers reluctant to use interactive whiteboards in their classroom?
12 Which teachers make very intensive use of interactive whiteboards?
13 Has the availability of interactive whiteboards changed the teaching style of teachers?
14 Are there factors currently inhibiting the use of interactive whiteboards in the classroom?
15 Which teachers have access to interactive whiteboards?
16 On what basis are teachers chosen to have access to interactive whiteboards?
17 Does the head teacher's attitude to interactive whiteboards influence their implementation in a school?
18 What changes in use of the interactive whiteboards have occurred since their introduction?
19 What views do pupils have about interactive whiteboards?
20 Would the money spent on interactive whiteboards be better spent on other things?

From Research Questions to a Research Design

The general topic of the use of interactive whiteboards (i.e. large screens on which the teacher can not only produce and show written material, but where pictures, DVDs, websites and interactive material can be displayed) in the school classroom, could be approached using many different research designs. The questions provide pointers to the design, and the type and style of the project.

Several of the questions, for example questions 2 to 5 inclusive, and 7 to 10 inclusive, suggest some kind of teacher survey. Question 11 might best be addressed by interviewing teachers. Question 1, and probably questions 12 and 14 to 17 inclusive and question 19, suggest some observational study in schools, coupled with interviews with pupils, teachers and the head teacher. Questions 13 and 18 would ideally call for some type of longitudinal study with researcher involvement in the school(s) for a period before the introduction of whiteboards and over the next year or so after their introduction.

Thinking about your splurged set of research questions helps you to take a step back and consider, not only the broad overall topic, but also what is going to be the purpose of your project. Perhaps you now appreciate that, at this stage at least, you just don't know enough about the situation in schools to do anything other than an exploratory study. This will effectively rule out a fixed design project and push toward flexible-style research.

However, if you have recent school experience, or find relevant research studies, then a fixed design project such as a survey or some kind of field experiment might well be feasible. Once decisions like this have been made, you can start pruning and generally tailoring your research question list so that it fits in with the focus you have, provisionally, decided on.

You still have more research question work to do. The main task is to decide which is the main research question (or questions). This doesn't stop you retaining some additional subsidiary questions, though you may well find that you have to drop some questions from the list at a later stage because you won't have the time and resources to get answers to them.

Do I really need research questions?

If you are working in a discipline such as psychology where there is a strong expectation that research questions are used (or even that you set up formal hypotheses – see the following section), you omit them at your peril. If you are working in other fields where there is no such strong expectation, it is more of a personal preference for particular ways of working. Some researchers find setting up research questions an unnecessarily constricting way of working. They prefer to decide on a focus of their research, go out and collect data; then see what they can make of what they have. Provided you follow the 'systematically/sceptically/ethically' rubric outlined at the start of chapter 2, p. 19, I wouldn't wish to warn you off following this tack. Certainly, you will find many published accounts of research which are not presented in terms of research questions.

However, I still hold firmly to the belief that the effort of sorting out some research questions, while it may be aversive, pays dividends. Provided you don't regard them as set in stone, where you have to stick with an initial set of questions, they can be adapted to virtually all styles of research from rigidly pre-specified designs to very flexible ones.

Don't forget that the purpose of the exercise is not just to get some research questions, but also to seek answers to them. It is not unknown for a report to list the questions, but not get round to providing an explicit discussion of the answers obtained as a result of doing the research.

Hypotheses

In some areas of research, there are strong traditions of talking in terms of hypotheses. In a general sense, 'having a hypothesis' about something means having a provisional, or tentative, explanation of what is going on. Thinking in this way can do nothing but good. It gives direction to your research and helps to suggest research questions.

However, there is a more restricted use of the term within the so-called hypothetico-deductive approach. Here the notion is that you start with a theory from which one or more hypotheses are derived. The central purpose of the research is to test the hypotheses. There can be a whole apparatus of null hypotheses and alternative hypotheses, often linked to an elaborate statistical technology for deciding between them. As I have already indicated, my own preference is to regard the research task as one of getting answers to questions rather than testing hypotheses. It has the advantage of applying to virtually all approaches to research, without straitjacketing you into one particular view of the nature of research.

It may be that you are researching in an area, or following an approach, where this hypothesis approach rules supreme. Your preparatory reading, particularly of journals, will reveal this – and if you are on a course, your supervisor will no doubt make this clear. If so, you had better go with the flow. Many standard texts give the rules (e.g. Coolican, 2004).

Developing the Design

Let's assume that, as a result of your preliminary reading and discussion with others (not least your supervisor), you have a pretty clear idea of the topic and focus of your project, of the approach you want to take, and that you have initial thoughts about research questions.

At this stage, the priority is to find out as much as you can about what others have already established, through research and review, relevant to your proposed project. This task forms the basis for the next section on finding and using sources. Be warned. It is not unknown for students to get so absorbed in searching for sources that they leave themselves insufficient time for actually carrying out the research, let alone writing it up.

You also need to give serious attention at this stage to the possible ethical implications of the proposed project. This is covered in the section following that on sources.

Finding and Using Sources

'Sources' are materials and people that can help you with your research project. The main concern here is to use such sources to give you ideas about how you should design your study. Has someone done a study that you can use as a model? Are there problems you haven't thought of? Or do you come across a study that leads to you thinking about the whole topic differently?

This isn't the only function of sources when doing a research project. For example, you will need them to provide backing for the claims you make when interpreting your data. Sources should inform every phase of the project and every aspect of your final report.

You are not alone when doing research, even though it may sometimes feel like that. The shadow army of all those who have done research and written about it is at your disposal. The trick is in finding relevant material. Your supervisor should help to get you going. Supervisors are, of course, themselves potentially very useful sources in their own right. This is particularly so if you are following a topic that they have suggested, and which links into their research interests. They should then be able to provide you with a set of key references that can save you much time and trouble.

The 'literature review' is often an expected part of a research report. It provides an account of previous research that has been carried out, together with attempts that have been made to provide frameworks within which the research can be placed and understood. All too often such reviews degenerate into an ill-digested listing of an inordinate number of references, which simply demonstrates that many more or less relevant sources have been unearthed by the writer. (The section on 'research arguments' in chapter 7, p. 142, makes suggestions about how you can structure the review.)

For my money, less can be more. In other words, there is greater value in homing in on a relatively small number of really key references and giving a full account of what they contribute and why it is relevant to your own study. However, if the powers that be insist on a review stuffed with many references, give them what they want! You should still ensure that you give sufficient space to do justice to what you consider to be the key references.

You will already have done some reading around when deciding on the topic of your research. If you are lucky, there might be one reference, perhaps a section in a book, or a review article on a particular field, or a journal account of a piece of research, which seems spot on.

Planning the search for sources

How do you start? Your efforts in deciding on a focus for the research will have thrown up an initial set of sources, whether suggested by your supervisor, or from books, research reviews, journal articles, newspapers or other media, or whatever. To take this further, there are two main avenues: the internet and libraries. You can get away with just using one of these if you have to. However, although the internet is an amazingly rich resource, I still find it easier to browse on the shelves of a library. Serendipity ('the happy knack of making fortunate discoveries') is a wonderful thing – the next book along on the shelf, or another paper in the journal rather than the one you were seeking, can prove to be a key source.

Key word searching Develop a set of key words to help you organize the search. Most journal articles include them. For example, an interview study on teachers' knowledge about adolescents (Adamson and Meister, 2005) included the following key words – adolescents, identity, teacher interviews, experiential knowledge, theoretical knowledge, teacher training, and school system. A case study of bullying at work (Matthiesen et al., 2003) included workplace bullying, work harassment, victimization, emotional abuse, interpersonal conflict, case study, conflict escalation model, and social support.

Using key words which seem obvious from the title of your project, together with ones that you glean from some relevant articles, should get you an initial set which you refine and modify as you go about your search. Many of the resources available via library catalogues or the internet make use of key word searching and you should make sure you can do this efficiently (there is usually a 'help' button which gives the rules).

A very basic rule which usually applies is that if you get too few 'hits' when using individual search terms, then try one key word '*or*' a second key word; if too many then a key word '*and*' a second one. If you find that a search returns many items of a particular type that you don't want, then use '*not*' to exclude them.

When you do come across relevant sources, do make sure that you get a full reference for them (e.g. for a journal reference you need the list of all authors and initials, title, journal name, year of publication, volume number and page numbers). A common style, used in psychology and several other disciplines and applied areas, is known as APA (American Psychological Association). The website gives details, together with details of, and references to, the styles used in other disciplines.

Partial references (e.g. where you have left out authors' initials or page numbers for a journal reference) are a pain when you are writing up. Just a few of them can cause you hours of work finding the missing details.

Internet searching

The business of getting hold of sources has been revolutionized in the last few years by the development of the internet. You can search for sources by traditional means using resources physically present in academic libraries. This kind of search still has a place, as discussed in the following section. However, it is perverse not to take advantage of the vast range of material now easily accessible via the internet.

It would be similarly perverse of me to devote many pages in this short text to giving suggestions on how to use the internet for research purposes, when excellent resources exist on the net itself to achieve this aim. For example, Intute (www.intute.ac.uk) provides a free service that guides you to peer-reviewed internet resources suitable for academic research. Simply browse the subject hierarchy to find a list of the key sources in your subject area. Intute: Social Sciences (formerly known as the Social Sciences Internet Gateway or SOSIG) is the social science branch of Intute and although United Kingdom based, it is not restricted to UK organizations or students, and includes links to US and other non-UK material.

A particularly valuable feature is the Intute Virtual Training Suite (www.vts. intute.ac.uk), a set of free online tutorials through which you can teach yourself essential internet research skills. There are over 60 tutorials covering social science subjects (including anthropology, business, development studies, economics, geography, government, law, psychology, social policy, social work, sociology, town and country studies and women's studies), health and life sciences (including agriculture, food and forestry, medicine, nursing, midwifery and health visiting, pharmacy, and veterinary studies), and the humanities (including English studies, history, religious studies and theology).

The tutorials cover not only key websites for each subject but also the best internet search tools and techniques. They provide training to deal with what is acknowledged to be the major problem in using the Web for research purposes – evaluating the quality of material from websites. One tutorial is devoted to social research methods and provides a valuable general resource for this text. Box 3.4 shows, as an example, some of the types of material covered. There is corresponding material in the other tutorials.

The box only covers three of nine categories of material dealt with in the tutorial. The tutorials also help you to evaluate for yourself other material you might find on the Web. Hence you should have the skills of discernment required when using a general search-engine such as Google (www.google. com). The 'academic' Google Scholar (www.scholar.google.com) can often turn up items not available in other searches including unpublished reports, conference proceedings and theses. These can contain the kind of detail on procedures not found in journal articles, which are particularly useful when designing a project. They need to be carefully evaluated from a quality point of

Box 3.4 Examples of material from the Intute Virtual Training Suite 'Internet for Social Research Methods' (www.vts.intute.ac.uk/tutorial/ social-research-methods)

Directories and Gateways

Gateways, directories and portals, all offer a structured entry point to a range of resources relating to a particular subject or field of interest.

Unlike search engines, which automatically collate a list of sites that match your search criteria, directories and gateways can provide a more fruitful search for your chosen topic. They have three main advantages:

☐ They have been put together by academic and library experts who have devoted much time to scanning the Web for items of interest.
☐ They have been arranged in structured and useful ways so that you can access the resources more easily.
☐ They are usually kept up to date on a regular basis

It is nice to know that there are easier ways to access information than random searches! The *discover* section will cover ways of searching on the internet in much more detail.

Gateways are an excellent place to go to find high quality internet sites that can support academic work.

☐ Intute: Social Sciences (formerly SOSIG), is the major UK gateway to internet resources in the social sciences. It has links to online papers, departments' and organizations' own Web pages, discussion lists, courses and more. There is a section devoted to Research Tools and Methods, featuring quantitative and qualitative resources. Furthermore, other discipline headings, such as psychology and anthropology, also have specific sections on research methods and methodology.
☐ Sociosite: Research Methodology and Statistics is a sociological information system based at the University of Amsterdam that gives access to a comprehensive and international listing of sociology related resources on the internet and has a special section devoted to research methodology and statistics.
☐ Social Science WWW Virtual Library which keeps track of online social science information as part of the World Wide Web Virtual Library.

Article Reference and Abstracts Database

Whether you are a teacher, student or researcher, you will often need to keep abreast of the latest publications in your field. The internet offers ways to find out about these publications via online catalogues of references and abstracts, some of which are freely available.

The following databases provide a good starting point for identifying publications about social research methods. They are also regularly updated.

However, please note that online access to some of these is through a higher educational institution only, for example, via ATHENS authentication. You should always consult your own library to see which ones they subscribe to and, where necessary, to obtain a password.

☐ The ISI Web of Knowledge Service for UK Education contains a number of useful reference products including: the Social Sciences Citation Index (SSCI) from the Web of Science which indexes around 5,000 journals spanning 50 social science disciplines that cover social research methods. You can access cited references and author abstracts going back to 1981; the 1945–1980 Back files for Web of Science cover cited references for the previous thirty years; the Journal Citation Reports (JCR) Social Sciences Edition contains data from roughly 1,500 multidisciplinary and international journals in the social sciences and the ISI Proceedings Social Science and Humanities edition (SSHP) that indexes the published literature of the most significant conferences and workshops across a wide range of disciplines from 1990.

☐ Z-Electronic Table of Contents (ZETOC) is a searchable database of the British Library's Electronic Table of Contents (ETOC). This includes around 20,000 current journals and around 16,000 conference proceedings published per year dating back to 1993, and is updated on a daily basis. It includes an e-mail alerting service.

☐ International Bibliography of the Social Sciences (IBSS) provides access to over 2 million bibliographic references to journal articles and to books, reviews and selected chapters dating back to 1951. Abstracts and full text are also increasingly being provided.

☐ CSA Sociological Abstracts – abstracts and indexes journal articles, book review citations, dissertations and conference papers since 1963 drawn from over 1,800 international serials publications across the social and behavioural sciences. There is a section on methodology and research technology. Access to CSA Sociological Abstracts also includes: ASSIA: Applied Social Sciences Index and Abstracts; Recent References Related to the Social Sciences/Humanities; and Web Resources Related to the Social Sciences/Humanities.

☐ FirstSearch offers electronic access to a range of databases and full-text and full-image articles, based on the WorldCat database. Included are Social Sciences Abstracts, Social Sciences Index, and the SIRS Researcher, covering records for articles selected from international newspapers, magazines, journals, and government publications.

Online Journals and Texts (part only)

The availability of online text allows quick and easy access to documents for which you would otherwise have to make a visit to the library and photocopy or request directly from the author or publisher.

The kinds of documents available on the internet include official and unofficial reports, publications, essays, reviews, on-going debates and press articles.

Online journals

Most journals in the social sciences have websites. Depending on the title of the electronic journal, you may be able to

☐ read the current full text online
☐ read the backdated full text online
☐ read tables of contents and/or abstracts only (current and backdated).

However, the catch is that for the majority of journals, gaining access to the full electronic text requires your institution to subscribe to the journal. You therefore need a username and password, such as ATHENS.

Below are some examples of online journals covering social research methods, but also note that many of the abstract services described earlier are also increasingly offering online text access.

Freely accessible full text peer-reviewed journals include:

☐ *Sociological Research Online* is an online journal that publishes high quality applied sociology articles, focusing on theoretical, empirical and methodological discussions.
☐ *Social Research Update* is a quarterly electronic journal that covers new developments in social research. Each issue covers a different research methods topic spanning qualitative and quantitative methods and it is pitched at a level that can be appreciated by both novice and expert reader.
☐ *The Qualitative Report* is an online journal dedicated to qualitative research and critical inquiry and which serves as a forum and sounding board for researchers, scholars and practitioners.
☐ *Forum for Qualitative Social Research* (FQS) is a free multilingual online journal for qualitative research that aims to promote discussion and

co-operation between qualitative researchers from different countries and social science disciplines.

You can check which journals and periodicals covering social research methods are available online by visiting:

☐ *Directories of Electronic Journals* provides links to Directories and Lists of Electronic Journals and Newsletters across the world.
☐ *The Journal and Article Locators in Psychology and the Social Sciences* which indexes more than 2,000 psychology and social science journals on the web and provides links to their home pages.
☐ *The Scholarly Journal Archive* (JSTOR) provides a full-text archive of scholarly journals starting with their first issues, and covers most of the social science disciplines. The collection covers materials from the 1880s up to a 'moving wall' of between 2 and 5 years.
☐ *Sociology*: A SAGE Full-Text Collections includes online access to over 125 SAGE journals, 40,000 articles, book reviews, and editorials, with original graphics and tables. Social research methods is well represented, dating back some 30 years.

Examples of journals of interest for social research methods which allow you to browse tables of contents and/or abstracts online are:

☐ *Sociological Methodology* is an annual volume on methods of research in the social sciences. Sponsored by the American Sociological Association, it publishes material that advances empirical research in sociology and related disciplines.
☐ *Qualitative Research* provides a forum for the discussion of research methods, in particular qualitative research, across the social sciences and cultural studies.
☐ *International Journal of Social Research Methodology* (IJSRM) is a new journal covering a mix of academic and theoretically slanted methodological articles and articles relating to research practice in professional and service settings.
☐ *Public Opinion Quarterly* (POQ) is the official publication of the American Association for Public Opinion Research (AAPOR) and focuses on theories and methods underlying opinion research such as survey validity, questionnaire construction, interviewing and interviewers, sampling and analytic approaches.
☐ *Quality & Quantity*: International Journal of Methodology provides an interdisciplinary forum for discussion on instruments of methodology for more rigorous scientific results in the social sciences. Issues covered

include causal analysis and classification, mathematical models, and the logic of empirical research.

Online texts

There are many sites now which provide electronic versions of text of interest to researchers. Examples are working paper series, conference proceedings, and media news. The texts are not necessarily peer reviewed or edited and the REVIEW section of the tutorial will address essential issues about the quality and reliability of these kinds of electronic sources.

Some sites publish full texts of academic papers on their websites:

☐ *Education Online: Electronic Texts in Education and Training* has an archive of full texts of papers given at educational research conferences.
☐ *The Centre for Microdata Methods and Practice* (cemmap) at the Institute for Fiscal Studies and the Department of Economics at University College London. Cemmap publishes working papers online that are freely downloadable.

Other organizations post up key documents such as ethical guidelines for research:

☐ *Medical Research Council (MRC) Ethics Series* which offers full texts of very detailed guidelines on ethics relating to medical research, including social research with patients.

view and are sometimes early drafts that have subsequently been modified on publication (search to see whether a published version exists).

Web-based discussion groups (sometimes referred to as listservs) are available for a vast number of research related areas. Many are freely accessible to all interested in the topic and members will often respond to requests for help in finding relevant material for a project. If you access 'Intute' mentioned above you will find a long list.

Library searching

One great thing that libraries have in their favour is librarians. They can lead you to the range of resources (including internet resources) available in and through the libraries. Subject librarians in academic libraries are often mines of information that will help you in your searches. Take advantage of any training courses going. Pick up leaflets on the different resources such as databases (e.g. BIDS, Web of Science, ERIC) including citation indices (e.g. SSCI – the Social Science Citation Index). Citation indices, available in print and in electronic versions, are useful in helping you to move forward. A reference you think is key to your project may well have been cited by others following its publication. A citation index lets you check this.

Books and print journals remain an important library resource. Keyword searches through the library catalogue will help you to find where relevant books are located. Inter-library loans will get you texts not in your own library, but can take time to come through. There is a multitude of journal article subject bibliographies through which you can search. There will probably be a small number of journals where many of the articles from your searches will be found. Have a good browse through the last few years' issues and particularly the 'current parts' which are often in a different part of a library. Revisit them when you are writing up as you may well find that something new has just been published that you should know about.

Asking the author

If you are finding it difficult to get access to a key reference from a journal or elsewhere, you can always try contacting the author. Use this tactic sparingly and don't just ask for lists of references. Affiliations of authors (i.e. where they are based) are usually provided in journals. If e-mail addresses are not given it is often not difficult to find them through an institution's website.

Dealing with the sources

Once you have found some sources (books, journal articles or whatever) which look promising, the next task is to sort them out in some way.

One approach is to sort them into three piles (either real or virtual piles depending on whether you are dealing with paper or electronic sources) – 'key', 'useful', and 'useless'.

Key sources are ones that are central to your topic and research questions. Perhaps ones that you can use as a model for your own efforts, or which suggest a next step. In my experience, you will be lucky to come up with more than half a dozen of these.

Useful sources are ones that you may want to take note of in some way, perhaps in the design of your project, or simply by referring to them in your report.

Useless sources are ones that on first glance looked relevant but further reading reveals that they aren't. Don't throw them away; your project might change and develop in ways that make them relevant. Keep them separately so that they don't clutter up your active set of sources.

Sorting a long list of 'possibles' can take a long time. Good reading skills help. If you are a slow reader, consider spending some time to increase your speed. (A Web search for 'speed reading' will throw up many possible approaches). Useful reading techniques include:

Skimming A rapid dash through the source to try to get an impression of whether there are any ideas or information you might use and to decide if it is relevant.

Scanning Another rapid dash but this time looking for a specific item. Does it have anything about X? You ignore everything else. (However I often find that something I wasn't looking for attracts my attention – and turns out to be valuable!)

Reading for understanding Once you have made the decision that a source is likely to be useful, possibly a key source, then you need to study it in some detail to ensure that you understand it. This study might be limited to a short passage, or a chapter in a book, or the whole of a journal article or book. For anything longer than a short passage, it helps to focus initially on what Booth et al. (2003; p. 106) call the geography of the source. For a book this means:

☐ reading the preface
☐ checking the contents table
☐ reading any introductions to chapters and chapter summaries (if there aren't any, skim through each chapter, noting the major sections it is divided into).

For a journal article this means:

☐ reading the abstract
☐ reading the introductory and concluding sections
☐ noting the major sections.

Now you have a feeling for the lie of the land, the hard work starts. While the source may not have actually set explicit research questions, an approach I find helpful is to ask what are the questions (or problems) they are trying to address? And what are the answers (or solutions) they have come up with? Some sources focus on a single main question, but there will typically be several subsidiary questions lurking around.

Note making You need to have a record of each source that you are likely to make use of. At a minimum, this involves the information to be included in the bibliography or reference list at the end of your report (see chapter 7, p. 147). *Make sure that you record and store this information for each source that you are likely to use, immediately that you decide it may be useful.* As already stressed, it can be a major pain, and cost much time and effort, to search for missing references when completing your report.

There is specialized bibliographic software (also known as 'reference managers'), such as EndNote or ProCite, which can be very helpful if you have to deal with a lot of references. They can capture electronically the reference details (and often the abstracts as well) of journal articles in e-journals, which can save much fiddly typing.

Making additional notes about a source is very much a personal decision. Some people feel that they never understand something unless and until they have expressed it in their own words. Others spend many happy, though probably largely pointless, hours highlighting or underlining large chunks of the source. This is mainly an issue with your small set of key references. You do need to know them well and undoubtedly you demonstrate this understanding to yourself and others by writing your own account. Such an understanding may be central to the way you design and carry out your project. However, it is in the report of the research that you have to incorporate discussion of the various sources and their relevance to your project, and you may be making better use of your precious time by writing drafts of parts of the report.

Ethical Considerations

Carrying out any form of research can have an effect on people in a wide variety of ways. Indeed, it might be argued that there is little point to research if it doesn't have the potential to affect someone in some way. Researchers are more likely to see the potential for good in their efforts, whether through increased understanding, more effective or efficient products, or some other positive contribution. However, even with entirely benign intentions, actual consequences can be negative, and possibly harmful, for those taking part in the research, or for those whose lives are affected by the results of the research. Unleashing the power of nuclear energy, or developing genetically modified crops, are commonly cited examples where researchers face difficult dilemmas.

While much social research does not generate such sharply polarized debate, the fact that it necessarily involves people, often in a very direct way as participants in the research, inevitably raises ethical issues. Have their rights, autonomy and sensitivities been respected? Is it possible that they will come to harm in some way as a result of their involvement? Do they know what they are letting themselves in for – in the jargon, have they given informed consent? Even just holding confidential information about another person has ethical implications.

It is, of course, not only the direct participants who might be affected by your research. Suppose your findings are used to justify the closure of a service or facility. Clients may suffer as a result. Or perhaps the findings are seen as justifying a new approach, which may be fine if you have shown its benefits, but less so if its attraction is primarily because it is cheap.

Possible ethical issues arising from your project should be discussed with your supervisor at an early stage. For example, what are you going to do if a participant becomes distressed in an interview? Sensitive topics where distress is likely should be avoided by novice researchers. However, apparently innocuous topics might turn out to be sensitive to some, and you need to be prepared (perhaps to stop the interview with an offer to talk it through if they would like to, or offer post-interview follow up).

It is good practice for there to be an 'ethics approval document' which has to be agreed with your supervisor, either making out the case for there being no ethical issues raised by the study, or giving details of the issues that are raised. In the UK it is likely to include a section on how you plan to meet the requirements of the Data Protection Act. Any ethical issues must then be thought through and the decision to proceed only made after it can be demonstrated that every effort has been made to reduce any likely harmful effects to a minimal level. These negative effects are likely to be outweighed by the potential benefits of the study. Who makes this decision? Certainly not you. Nor should this be a decision made by researchers on their research proposals, even if they are vastly more experienced than you are. The website gives examples of documents used in relation to ethical approval, including checklists covering the issues that need to be addressed in relation to the Data Protection Act.

Ethics committees

It is increasingly common for there to be a formal committee set up with this responsibility, possibly combining this with more general powers of approval for the research proposal. Your supervisor should know the set-up and give advice about what is needed. Some types of proposal will need the approval of more than one ethics committee (e.g. if you are working for an award at an academic institution but carrying out the research in a hospital or other health-related setting). This can be a pain if different committees have different requirements, or if a committee has little experience of small-scale undergraduate projects. Your supervisor should seek to sort this out and to establish where it goes first.

If you are working under your own steam, or are carrying out the research as part of your job in an organization, you need to get support. Certainly consult relevant sets of ethical guidelines (see below) to ensure that you appreciate the issues involved. You then need to check out your proposals with potential participants and other stakeholders, such as management, unions, clients of a service and, if at all possible, someone, perhaps in a college, with experience of evaluating ethical concerns. In a work setting, you need to satisfy yourself that the sponsors of the study wish this to be carried out for ethically reputable reasons and are not using you to legitimize something disreputable.

Ethical guidelines

Almost all disciplines and fields of study have approved sets of ethical guidelines. In the UK, examples include those developed by the British Association of Social Workers, the British Educational Research Association, the British Psychological Society, the British Sociological Association, the Medical Research Council, the Royal College of Nursing and the Social Research Association. Other countries have similar sets of guidelines. You should consult the relevant one – links to several examples are provided on the website. Particular types of research are likely to raise specific ethical issues (for example, insider research where you are already a member of the institution or organization which forms the focus of your project can pose difficult ethical dilemmas – see chapter 5, p. 104).

Avoiding the unethical

Things that might be considered dubious on ethical grounds include:

☐ involving people without their knowledge, or without their explicit and informed consent
☐ exerting pressure to become involved in the research
☐ using deception about the purpose of the research, or what taking part involves
☐ exposing participants to ridicule or embarrassment, or otherwise injuring their self-esteem
☐ putting participants under physical or mental stress
☐ invading privacy or not respecting participants' autonomy, e.g. when seeking to change behaviour, attitudes, etc.
☐ giving benefits or rewards to some but not others
☐ treating people unfairly, or with lack of consideration or respect.

It is, however, difficult to sustain the argument that each of these practices should always be avoided. There are public situations where it is not feasible to ask for consent, nor to ensure that people even know that they are being focused on in a study (for example, in studies of car driver behaviour at traffic lights, or in the vicinity of speed cameras). Is the pressure exerted on students in some psychology degree courses to act as participants in departmental research projects, unethical? Or is it legitimized as a social commitment appropriate for members of that department?

In some fields, notably social psychology, deception as to the purposes of the research is used. The argument put forward is that knowing the real purpose would preclude study of the phenomenon researched. Outright deception to the extent of lying is rarely proposed in current research. A softer and more acceptable line involving 'honest but vague on details' is now more commonly taken. For example, a study focusing on which students talk in 'quiet' areas of a university library might be advised to present the project as 'interested in student use of the library' when conducting interviews. (This would be quite tricky to design. Do you observe first, then interview? Do you interview 'talkers' and 'non-talkers'? How do you define them? Where and when do you interview – presumably not in the quiet area?) More generally, there is a welcome change of climate where what might be termed 'participants' rights' are taken more seriously. This is particularly so in research involving vulnerable groups such as children and persons with disabilities. However, horror stories still occur and there is a continuing need for vigilance

The website provides links covering issues to be considered when doing an ethical health-check on your proposed research. There are also links to examples of informed consent letters and suggestions for the procedures that might be followed to ensure that there is 'true' informed consent rather than just jumping through a procedural hoop.

Confirming Your Choices

Reading the material from the sources you have obtained, together with more thinking and discussion, should help you to firm up the likely detailed focus of your project. Does it look as if you will have to do an exploratory study because little relevant research appears to be available? There is nothing wrong with doing this type of study, but is it something that you would feel comfortable with? If not, you will need to rethink and refocus on an area where there is previous work that you can build on.

Has the reading confirmed what you thought were your main research question(s) or do you now consider something rather different would be more appropriate? As discussed earlier in the chapter (p. 51), the form of these questions provides pointers to the design.

Further Reading

Andrews, R. (2003) *Research Questions*. London and New York: Continuum. Short but informative guide to developing research questions.
Blaikie, N. (2000) *Designing Social Research: The logic of anticipation*. Cambridge:

Polity Press. Emphasis on the formulation of research questions and selection of appropriate approach to research.

Gregory, I. (2003) *Ethics and Research*. London and New York: Continuum. Reviews the ethical concerns that underlie all aspects of carrying out a research project.

Smith, M. and Williamson, E. (2004) *Researchers and Their Subjects*. Bristol: The Policy Press. Case studies of proposals where ethical issues were central. Covers a wide range of disciplines.

Van Den Hoonaarch, W. C. (2002) *Walking the Tightrope: Ethical issues for qualitative researchers*. Toronto: University of Toronto Press. Focus on ethical issues specific to qualitative research.

Zeni, J. (2001) *Ethical Issues in Practitioner Research*. New York: Teachers College Press. Ethical problems in action research and insider studies.

Chapter 3 Tasks

Following discussions with your supervisor, with colleagues (in the group if you've managed to set one up) and your initial reading:

1 Firm up your choice of topic for the project. You can still change it if, after further reading and thought, you don't think it will work out. But beware of wasting time over this.
2 Write down a 'long list' of possible research questions. Think of as many as you can in, say, half an hour. Invite suggestions and comments.
3 Consider what kind of approach (case study, survey, etc.) might be appropriate for the different questions. You should be able to group together questions that would call for the same approach.
4 Decide, provisionally, on the main research question or questions. Choose something which can be tackled by an approach you feel comfortable with, which will be feasible within your time and resource constraints, and which you find interesting.
5 Find out as much as you can relevant to the topic and the research question(s). Chase up relevant sources via the library and internet. The purpose of this search is to get ideas for the design of the project and to assess whether the provisional decisions you have made about focus and research questions need modifying. Set a time limit of a few days for this search (there's a danger that this gets so involving that you do not want to stop – don't forget that you actually have to carry out the project and write it up as well).
6 Revisit your earlier decisions in the light of the search, and come up with a working title.
7 Review ethical issues. Write down the possible issues (using a pro-forma if available) and discuss them with your supervisor. Take advice about the need for formal ethical approval procedures.
8 Consider whether it will be necessary to obtain access to do the research. Take advice from your supervisor on this and on how access is to be requested. As obtaining agreement for access can be a lengthy process, start it as soon as possible (see chapter 5, p. 100).

4

Selecting the Method(s) of Collecting Data

The next task, after you have:

☐ decided on a topic
☐ selected a focus, or aspect, of the topic which you're going to concentrate on
☐ sorted out a set of research questions (which you may, or may not, stick with – depending on how things work out)
☐ worked out your design in general terms (which will include the style or approach which seems best fitted to approach the topic and answer the research questions) and
☐ given serious thought to the ethical issues involved

is to decide on your main method of data collection.

For small-scale projects, it is usually best to make one method central to the project. Perhaps it's essentially an interview-based project or mainly based on postal questionnaires, or whatever. Experiments typically have specialized methods specific to particular topics. Focusing your efforts on one method means that you can afford to spend the time needed to get on top of the practicalities of its use.

However, even in a small project, there is much to be said for devoting a small proportion of your time and effort to collecting data by some different method. This will almost inevitably give you a somewhat different perspective on the data you get from the main method. In research jargon, this is called triangulation of methods, after the way in which a surveyor gets a 'fix' on position by approaching it from different angles.

One straightforward combination is to have documentary analysis as a secondary data collection method. In many situations, when doing research outside the laboratory it helps to have 'sticky fingers' where you pick up copies of various documents in the setting where your project is based. Unless these are freely available documents (such as a prospectus, booklet or leaflet), you must get permission of course.

It is also often possible to conduct some relatively informal interviews as a secondary method. Incorporating this type of data collection into a laboratory experiment, for example, can with little cost of time and effort, give a valuable participant's perspective on the experiment.

Trustworthiness and Credibility

Whatever data collection method, or methods, that you use, you need to have a defence against a reader (or examiner!) who asks 'Why should I believe you?' when looking at your data and the way you have interpreted the findings.

I assume that, as stressed in chapter 2, p. 18, you are approaching this task seriously and honestly. Any cheats who make up or fiddle data, please leave now.

How do you seek to persuade the reader that what you are saying is worthy of trust? Your account is credible, or believable, largely through the general quality of the account that you provide, including full details of what you did, and why you did it. There are, traditionally, two specific concerns associated with the data you collect. Are they reliable? Are they valid?

Reliability

Data collection is reliable if you get essentially the same data when a measurement is repeated under the same conditions. If you start thinking about how this might be assessed, some logical and practical problems come to the fore. It is virtually impossible to get an exact repetition of a measurement when you are working with people. Even when using a highly standardized method such as a questionnaire or some type of test, a question asked again to see if you get the same response has logically to be at a different time. By then the situation, or your respondent, may have changed in some way. The very fact that a question is repeated may lead to a different answer out of perversity or boredom.

When using standardized methods of data collection, it is usually feasible to get some reasonable reassurance about reliability. For example, using structured observation it is possible to have two observers. The test is whether or not they produce very similar results independently when observing the same situation. This is known technically as high inter-observer reliability. To get to this stage, it is often necessary to train observers for lengthy periods. When questionnaires or scales are used, it is possible to have alternative versions of the questions or test items that you try to make sure are equivalent. Again, if the two versions produce essentially equivalent patterns of data from those responding, it demonstrates reliability.

Researchers who prefer flexible designs, and the use of methods that produce qualitative data, can consider the whole idea of reliability somewhat dubious. They argue that they are dealing with complex and messy real-life situations, where highly standardized data collection methods are neither appropriate nor feasible. Accepting the force of this argument still leaves readers legitimately worried about whether they can rely on the data that have been collected. Tactics such as providing very full 'thick' descriptions, which include the context in which observations are made, provide some reassurance. The use of triangulation (e.g. collecting data by different methods, from different informants and from different types of informant) can also help.

Validity

Validity refers to whether or not something actually measures what it claims to measure. A measure can be reliable without being valid. For example, a test that purports to measure suitability for a particular job might be highly reliable in that the same people get the same scores when tested twice, but be useless at predicting later performance on the job. If it's not reliable, it can't be valid.

Validity is a worry whatever approach or method is used. There are technical, often complex, methods for assessing various types of validity when structured data collection methods are used. When using flexible designs and qualitative methods, are you telling the 'truth'? In other words, does your account fairly and accurately represent the phenomenon or situation? Or are the selections and interpretations you have made in some way biased, perhaps reinforcing a particular agenda?

See the 'big' research methods texts in the further reading at the end of the chapter for details on the procedures you need to follow to ensure that your methods are reliable and your conclusions valid.

Research arguments

Above and beyond these technical issues, you answer the 'Why should I believe that?' question by the quality of the research argument presented in the report of your findings. This is the claim you make (typically in the form of answers to the research questions), linked to the evidence and reasons you present. It is discussed in detail in the final chapter.

However, in order to be in a position to present this argument in the report, you need to anticipate having to do this throughout the research process. It helps if you work at a draft of the report at an early stage. Much research is confirmatory. That is, you have a pretty good idea of what your findings are likely to be before the complete data are collected. This puts the onus on you to look actively for contrary evidence, i.e. findings that will contradict or disconfirm your expectations. Anticipating possible findings helps you to home onto the kinds of evidence that will strengthen your research argument, and to make sure that you look for this evidence while collecting data.

Even in a flexible exploratory study, where you don't have strong prior expectations, early data collection will begin to throw up ideas about the likely findings. It helps to shape the ways in which your data collection evolves. Again, your task is to try to collect data that will support the research argument you will eventually present.

Data Collection Methods

The following sections on data collection methods or techniques give sufficient detail for you to get a feeling for what is involved in a range of commonly used methods. Suggestions for further readings are given at the end of each section. They provide the detailed information you will need if you decide to use one of the methods in your project.

Interviews

The heart of the interview technique is one person (the interviewer or researcher) talking to one or more other persons (the interviewees or participants). The most common format is the individual, face-to-face interview. However, group interviews of various types can be very valuable in some projects. The telephone interview is increasingly favoured, as it retains some of the advantages of direct person-to-person interaction, while often substantially decreasing the travelling and time commitment called for in face-to-face interviews.

There are many types of research interview. One of the ways in which they differ is in the amount of structure, ranging from fully structured to totally unstructured.

Fully structured interviews

The fully structured interview is essentially a structured questionnaire where the questions are put by the interviewer, usually face-to-face, who then notes the answers. Questions are typically 'closed', in the sense that there is a set of possible alternative answers from which the interviewee has to choose. In any questions where the answer is not restricted in this way, the interviewer is usually asked to code the response according to a predetermined set of alternatives.

Genuinely 'open' questions are kept a minimum, and are often restricted to the 'Anything further you would like to say?' type asked at the end of the interview.

In fully structured interviews, most of the thinking work is carried out up-front, before the interview itself. The questions are not just those that you think it might be interesting to ask, nor are they the research questions themselves. They are questions that are going to help you get answers to the research questions. Because fully structured interviews are effectively the same as structured questionnaires, the comments made on questionnaires (p. 79 below) apply.

The advantage of using an interview situation is that it is usually easier to get a high response rate (by comparison with a postal, or similar non-face-to-face situation). People find it more difficult to say no, or to give up, if you are with them – particularly if you have good social skills. It is also possible to judge the seriousness with which they take the exercise, which can be helpful in interpretation.

Semi-structured interviews

In this type of interview, you as researcher work out in advance not only the overall focus of the interview but also the main areas that you want to cover, together with the sequence in which you want to cover the areas. Write out the topics on a card that you can refer to in the interview. You may also, particularly as a novice – and possibly nervous – interviewer, feel more confident if you have written down a form of wording for the questions.

However, you have considerable freedom when doing semi-structured interviews. While you will probably stick to pre-planned initial and final questions (starting off with non-threatening, unlikely to be sensitive ones, and ending with an opportunity for them to add things which they feel you may have missed), you can change the planned sequence depending on how things are going. If the interviewee comments on something you had planned to cover later, you don't choke them off. Go with it. If something is disturbing, you don't follow it up with something likely to be more so. Move on to something else and return later.

Similarly, you don't need to use an exact question wording (as you should in a fully structured interview). If handled well, the semi-structured interview can almost sound like a conversation between two people. This naturalism will help to put the interviewees at their ease and probably get you more helpful and informative answers.

However, it should actually be a carefully controlled interaction, where you have an agenda that you need to follow. Some researchers find this socially difficult. There is a fine balance to be struck between encouraging interviewees to talk freely, and them treating it as an opportunity to have a cosy chat. You need to be able to steer them back without destroying the rapport you have built up.

By comparison with the fully structured interview, you have substantially less preparatory work, but the conduct of the interview itself is a more demanding task. It's something you need practice at, calling for substantial pilot work until you feel reasonably confident at being able to carry it off. You also need to get a feel for whether or not the questions are helping you to get answers to your research questions.

Taping the interview is strongly recommended. There is enough to concern yourself with, without having to write their answers down (which also is likely to disturb the flow of the interview). You must ask permission to do this. Don't make a big thing of it. Something like 'Is it ok if I tape this? If I don't, I find it very difficult to remember everything' will usually be effective.

Don't forget that you not only have to budget for the time taken by the interview itself (rarely less than half an hour, say 45 minutes on average), and any travelling time to and from the place of the interview, but also the time taken to analyse the tape afterwards. If you are producing transcripts yourself, which you will probably have to unless you have an audio-typist to hand, it can take anything up to ten hours to get a good transcript for each hour of the interview. You don't, necessarily, have to make a full transcript. It may be sufficient to listen carefully to the recording and make notes, just transcribing (or noting the position on the tape of) interesting or important parts of the recording.

The analysis of their answers is also likely to take time and effort. It may be appropriate to seek to fit them into predetermined categories but it is much more likely, as in using a grounded theory approach (see chapter 2, p. 39, and chapter 6, p. 132), that the categories will be at least partially derived from the answers themselves.

Given that interviews seem to be appropriate for your study, the semi-structured version is often the best bet. While, as indicated above, this type of interview calls for a fair amount of practice to be reasonably confident in its use, the skills are not difficult to acquire, and are likely to be useful for you in later life in a range of job situations. Similarly, analysis of the resulting data, while time-consuming, is relatively straightforward.

Unstructured interviews

Unstructured interviews are, in my view, normally best avoided by novice researchers. Certainly, putting all your research methods eggs into this type of interview is a very risky business. They come in various types, including the depth interview, which has similarities to some psychotherapy interviews (though carried out with a research rather than a therapeutic intent).

In the unstructured interview, virtually all the work and thought on your part goes into the interview itself. You have, at most, an overall focus for the interview. In the hands of a skilled and experienced interviewer who is able to follow the leads given by the interviewee and to turn them to research account, it can produce rich and complex data. But it is a difficult option for a first research project.

In many projects, there can, however, be considerable value in informal interviews. This is where, while using a different main research method (say, participant observation), you take opportunities that arise to have short interviews in the setting you have been observing. They can be focused, where you might be seeking clarification as to what was going on in something you have just watched. Or they can just be regarded as an opportunity to chat, which may bring up something you find useful or enlightening. Such interviews can help to 'humanize' you in the eyes of participants and possibly reduce the reactive effect of your 'researcher' presence.

Group interviews

Group interviews can be an efficient way of obtaining data from several people at the same time. They can provide a relatively low-cost way (in terms of your time and effort) of getting a feel for the important issues in a new field of research. If well managed they can be a safe way of exploring controversial issues, as long as confidentiality can be assured and trust established. However, they can be tricky to conduct. Some people tend to hog the limelight, others won't open their mouth. Trying to ensure that everyone contributes, while keeping the situation relatively informal, will test your social skills. It can also be very difficult to capture what everyone says. Taping is essential and it is not straightforward to get an adequate recording of each contributor's voice; nor to recognize individual voices reliably. If possible, it is a good idea to have a second person helping you. You run the interview and the second person handles the taping and the making of back-up notes. A dummy run with friends can be helpful.

Group interviews give you the views of the group. What you get is not necessarily the same as you would have got from individual interviews. This has advantages as it provides the opportunity for individuals to react to the views of others, either giving their support or expressing a different view. Group solidarity can allow buried issues to come to the surface. A disadvantage is that the dynamics of the group will influence the outcome in ways specific to that group.

Focus groups are a widely used type of group interview, particularly popular in marketing and advertising, and in divining the views of the electorate by political parties. They call for quite tight control by the person running the group and, as the name suggests, are typically focused on a specific issue. Rather prescriptive, and detailed, rules for the conduct of focus groups have been developed (see the book by Litosseliti in the further reading list below for details).

Telephone interviews

The telephone interview is becoming increasingly popular as a research tool. It has many of the advantages of the face-to-face interview, though perhaps in a rather watered-down way. For example, it is possible to establish empathy when having a phone conversation, although, because of the absence of non-verbal cues, it's not as easy as when you are in the same room as the interviewee. Providing you have established a prior contact and got over to them what the research is about, and made it clear that you are not cold-calling to sell double-glazing, most people are prepared to be involved.

The big advantage is in the use of your precious time. The travelling time is zero. Both structured and semi-structured types are feasible over the phone. With the latter you will probably need to record the interview and must, of course, get prior permission to do this. Recording needs specialised equipment to do it properly. As body language and other non-verbal cues are lost, telephone interviewing is not suitable for less structured types of interview. Box 4.1 lists some of the advantages and disadvantages of interviews.

Box 4.1 Some advantages and disadvantages of interviews

Advantages

1 They are a research version of something you do all the time – talking to people. Provided you like talking to people (often strangers), it can be enjoyable.
2 There is usually relatively little resistance to being interviewed (by comparison with other methods, such as asking them to complete questionnaires). Hence there is rarely a problem in achieving high response rates.
3 No special equipment is needed apart from a good tape-recorder and microphone.
4 The face-to-face situation gives you the opportunity to develop empathy with the interviewee, which can help in getting better, fuller, responses and increase the chance that they will take the questions seriously.
5 This also gives you the chance of assessing the value of the answers, through non-verbals, throw-away comments, etc.
6 There are different types of interview, so you can select a style appropriate for many different approaches to research including both fixed and flexible designs.

Disadvantages

1 It can be difficult to keep 'on topic', especially if you are both enjoying the interview.
2 They can take up a lot of time, particularly if you have to travel (consider telephone interviews if this is a problem).
3 You need good social skills to interview well.
4 They either require much preparation and piloting (with more structured interviews) or call for well-developed research skills and experience (with less structured interviews).
5 Apart from highly structured interviews (where the analysis is usually straightforward), they usually need to be taped, followed by lengthy transcription and analysis.
6 They are subject to bias (e.g. interviewees are likely to say what they think you want to hear, or puts them in a good light).

Using interviews in your project

If you are going to use interviews as a data collection method, you are recommended to follow up one or more of the further reading texts below to get a detailed understanding of what is involved. The website gives links to other relevant websites.

Further reading

Arksey, H. and Knight, P. T. (1999) *Interviewing for Social Scientists: An introductory resource with examples.* London and Thousand Oaks. Useful introduction covering all the main approaches to interviewing.

Drever, E. (2003) *Using Semi-structured Interviews in Small-scale Research.* Glasgow: The SCRE Centre. Practical short text. Very useful if you know that you will be using semi-structured interviews.

Litosseliti, L. (2003) *Using Focus Groups in Research.* London: Continuum. Covers their benefits and limitations as well as practical details on all aspects of focus group research.

Rubin, I. and Rubin, H. J. (2004) *Qualitative Interviewing: The art of hearing data.* London and Thousand Oaks, CA: Sage. Covers all the steps of a qualitative interviewing project in a practical manner. Focus is on building confidence in beginning researchers so they can begin to interview right away.

Questionnaires and Diaries

Questionnaires

The questionnaire is probably the most widely used data collection method in social research, often in conjunction with a sample survey. As a jobbing researcher, it is not uncommon to get asked by a client 'Can you do me a questionnaire on . . .?' This puts the data collection method cart before the research question horse. In other words, the prior issue should be to sort out the research questions, then to decide if using questionnaires is actually the best way of getting answers to them. If you are absolutely determined to use questionnaires, then you will have to tailor your research questions appropriately.

Questionnaires are popular with novice researchers as they look quite straightforward. String a few questions together and post them to a particular target audience. Sit back and await replies. Turn their answers into numbers. Analyse them, and that's it. However . . . even if you get a good response rate (and postal questionnaires are notorious for having poor ones) which gives satisfying quantitative data, the data are highly likely to be close to meaningless.

To begin at the beginning. Most questionnaires are composed of items (usually, but not necessarily, questions; they can be statements to which they have to make a response) where choice has to made from a fixed set of alternatives (e.g. 'yes', 'no', or 'don't know'). Sometimes, a write-in response is asked for. The researcher afterwards codes the responses into predetermined categories. Using open questions where you haven't decided in advance how responses are to be categorized can store up a lot of trouble for you later.

Sorting out the wording of the questions requires considerable thought. They need to fulfil the twin requirements of helping you to get answers to the research questions, and being worded so that they are clear and unambiguous to participants. Most of this is common sense. Things like avoiding negatively phrased questions (which are more difficult to understand), double-barrelled questions (two questions in one), and leading questions (where the wording pushes toward a particular answer). The texts on questionnaires in the further reading below cover in detail the things you need to think about when designing questionnaires.

Because most of the effort with questionnaires is up-front in designing and presenting them professionally, it isn't usually sensible to use them with small samples. Also, as they typically generate quantitative data, or responses which can easily be turned into numbers, there need to be adequate numbers of responses to carry out an appropriate statistical analysis (see chapter 6, p. 164).

While postal questionnaires might be simplest from your point of view, they have many disadvantages. Apart from the difficulty in getting a satisfactory response rate (you can bump this up by things like making the questionnaire attractively and professionally presented, and sending at least two reminders, appropriately spaced in time, to non-respondents), you have little or no control over the seriousness with which they treat the task. Simply because you have a response which can be coded into a number does not guarantee that it is anything other than a semi-random set of box-ticks.

If resources permit, there is considerable advantage to administering the questionnaire in an interview situation (see section above on structured interviews, p. 73). If this isn't feasible, you might be able to set up the self-completion questionnaire exercise at a time when you are actually around. For example, if you're focusing on an educational setting, visit the school on the afternoon when they have agreed to ask their pupils to complete the questionnaire. Be around to oversee what is going on, sort out any glitches and collect the completed questionnaires before you leave. Try to set it up so that it is difficult for them to escape without letting you have their completed questionnaire – perhaps by collecting them while standing at the only exit door.

The need to get a high response rate has to be balanced by your making sure that people understand that they have the right not to complete the questionnaire (see section on ethics in chapter 3, p. 64).

Box 4.2 lists some of the advantages and disadvantages of questionnaires.

Diaries

This refers to diaries that you ask participants in your research to complete for you – not the research diary that you have for your own purposes (see chapter 1, p. 16).

Diaries are, from the researcher's perspective, a low-cost method of data collection and are well worth considering as a secondary, or subsidiary, data collection method. Participants are asked to complete an entry on a regular basis, typically daily but sometimes weekly or less frequently. Entries can take many forms but usually the same small set of items are to be completed each time. Often there are both questions and rating scales (rate your feelings about *x* on a 1 to 5 scale, where 1 is . . ., etc.).

As with postal questionnaires, you have little control over the seriousness with which the diary entry task is carried out, or indeed whether it is completed as specified, or all in one go when it is time to return the diary! Hence they are not advisable as the single, or main, data collection method. However, for some research topics, particularly those that respondents find involving, they can provide rich supporting data.

Diaries are particularly prone to what are sometimes called the 'demand characteristics' of the research situation, That is, a potential bias to responses from participants seeking to show themselves in a favourable light. For example, a recent survey asked university faculty members to complete diary entries detailing the extent to which they are involved in work-related activities while

Box 4.2 Some advantages and disadvantages of questionnaires

Advantages

1 It is possible to deal with a large sample even if you have relatively small resources (applies particularly to postal questionnaires).
2 The use of pre-coded answers simplifies the task of analysis.
3 They do not require personal interaction skills on the part of the researcher.
4 The absence of face-to-face interaction between researcher and participants reduces the effect of the researcher on responses.

Disadvantages

1 It can be very difficult to obtain acceptably high response rates. Efforts to improve response rates can involve substantial additional time and resources.
2 It is not possible to go into topics in depth, as long and complex questionnaires reduce response rates.
3 Checking the truthfulness of answers, or assessing the seriousness with which participants have approached the task, calls for sophisticated psychometric techniques (e.g. the development of 'lie' and 'social desirability' scales).
4 A good questionnaire calls for careful planning and design and meticulous attention to detail at all phases of the research.
5 The resulting quantitative data and associated statistical analysis can give an inflated impression of the value of the findings.

at home. Unsurprisingly (particularly as this was linked to a salary claim), most recorded very extensive activity.

Using questionnaires or diaries in your project

If you are going to use questionnaires or diaries as a data collection method, you are recommended to follow up one or more of the further reading texts below to get a detailed understanding of what is involved. The website gives links to other relevant websites.

Further reading

Alaszewski, A. (2006) *Using Diaries for Social Research*. London and Thousand Oaks, CA: Sage. Accessible introductory text. Covers structuring of diaries for research purposes and approaches to analysis.

Frazer, L. and Lawley, M. (2001) *Questionnaire Design and Administration: A practical guide.* Brisbane: Wiley. Very clear step-by-step instructions with good range of detailed examples.

Munn, P. and Drever, E. (2004) *Using Questionnaires in Small-scale Research.* Glasgow: The SCRE Centre. Short and very practical.

Oppenheim, A. N. (2000) *Questionnaire Design.* 3rd edition. London: Continuum. Latest edition of deservedly popular and very comprehensive text.

Tests and Scales

Intelligence and personality tests of various kinds are widely known. You will also almost certainly have come across tests in magazines claiming to tell you things about yourself – 'How gay are you?' was the latest I saw in yesterday's newspaper.

Tests can be a useful research tool. They enable you to get a measure of people's views, abilities, attitudes or opinions, and many other things. The tests produce a scale, usually numerical, on which you can place and compare individuals. There are hundreds of such tests, many of which are readily available (see the website for sources). Some, however, are only accessible to those holding professional qualifications in areas such as clinical, educational or occupational psychology.

Test construction is a highly technical matter. It is not acceptable, for research purposes, simply to come up with the list of questions which seem to you to be relevant to the topic of the research, say, people's attitudes to animal experimentation, and then derive a score in some way from their responses. Issues of reliability, and in particular validity (does it actually measure what I claim that it does? – see p. 71) loom large.

The amount of time needed to acquire the necessary skills in test construction effectively rules out your producing your own tailor-made test. Unless of course you already have the skills, or have someone to hand who will do it for you.

Realistically then, if you want to use a formal test in your project, you will almost certainly have to pick one off the shelf. Unfortunately, while there are many existing tests, it usually turns out that no available test does exactly what you need for your project. They either give answers to somewhat different questions to the ones you are after or they have been developed using, say, adults rather than the children you want to work with.

Don't be tempted to tinker with the published test or its questions. This invalidates the test as a research instrument. It may be possible for you to modify your intentions somewhat so that there is a closer fit between the available test and your research.

Box 4.3 lists some of the advantages and disadvantages of using tests and scales.

Box 4.3 Some advantages and disadvantages of using tests and scales

Advantages

1 They can be used to measure many different 'people' things, including attitudes, views, abilities, opinions, etc.
2 They are usually easy to administer, producing a numerical scale value on which people can be compared.
3 There is a wide range of existing tests which can be picked 'off the shelf', many of which have been developed by experts in the field.

Disadvantages

1 Devising a new test for research purposes is complex and time-consuming.
2 Existing tests will often not be exactly right for your purposes.
3 Many of the best tests may be expensive, or have restricted availability (i.e. they can only be used by those with particular professional qualifications).
3 'Test-aversion' is increasingly common in some groups.
4 Some tests may be viewed as threatening or sensitive, raising strong ethical issues and also affecting their acceptability.

Using tests or scales in your project

If you are going to use tests or scales as a data collection method, you are recommended to follow up one or more of the further reading texts below to get a detailed understanding of what is involved. The website gives links to other relevant websites, along with references to research projects using tests and scales in different disciplines and areas of research.

Further reading

Kline, P. (1999) *Handbook of Psychological Testing*. 2nd edition. London: Routledge. Revised edition of a standard text on testing.

Loewenthal, K. (2001) *An Introduction to Psychological Tests and Scales*. 2nd edition. London: Psychology Press. Revised version of a detailed and accessible introductory text.

Urbina, S. (2004) *Essentials of Psychological Testing*. Chichester: Wiley. Covers the main areas you need to consider when using tests in a project.

Observation – Structured and Participant

Structured observation

Observation involves watching people in some situation and making a record of what you have seen. As used in research, two very different styles are widely used. In structured observation, commonly used in studies of animal behaviour, an observation schedule is devised. This requires the observer to make decisions about how to categorize what she sees. Typically, there is a fixed set of possible alternative categories. Substantial training of observers is needed before such a schedule can be used reliably

The situation is very similar to the use of tests as a research instrument. While there are many published observation schedules, it is rare to find one that does exactly the job that you want done. Devising your own is a very difficult task. It is actually rather worse than with tests as, even if you find an existing observation schedule that is just right, you are still faced with a lengthy training period before you can use it reliably. To demonstrate that you are using it reliably you have to get a colleague or other researcher to help you by observing at the same time and cross-checking your use of the categories.

Box 4.4 lists some of the advantages and disadvantages of using structured observation.

Box 4.4 Some advantages and disadvantages of using structured observation

Advantages

1 It can be used to observe and analyse a very wide range of situations.
2 It provides a record of what people actually do, rather than what they say that they do (as in interviews and questionnaires).
3 There is a wide range of existing structured observation schedules that can be picked 'off the shelf'.
4 If you can find an existing schedule appropriate for your research, you can generate quantitative data of known reliability and validity.
5 It produces coded quantitative data that can be quickly and easily analysed.
6 The use of very clearly defined observational categories reduces the subjectivity and bias found in unstructured observation.

Disadvantages

1 Devising your own observation schedule is complex and time-consuming.
2 Existing observation schedules will often not be exactly right for your purposes.

---

3 Even if you find the 'right' schedule, it will take time and effort to be proficient in its use.

4 You need to demonstrate that you have achieved acceptably high standards of reliability in its use, usually through having a colleague provide independent observations.

5 Reactivity (the effects of the observer on what is happening) can be a serious problem.

6 It oversimplifies and decontextualizes complex situations, as only a small number of easily observable behaviours can be captured in observation schedules.

Participant observation

As the term suggests, participant observation is defined by the role taken by the observer. He, to some greater or lesser extent, actually participates in the situation being observed. It is an approach originating in anthropology, where it is closely linked to ethnography, but it is now popular in many areas of social research. There is a range of possibilities. At one extreme, the complete participant. Here the researcher is effectively just another member of the group involved. In some situations, this is done in a covert manner; i.e. the researcher does not reveal that he is observing the group for research purposes. This raises serious ethical issues. Justification has been claimed as this being the only way in which the research could be carried out. For example, it is fair to assert that it isn't feasible to reveal one's research intentions before participating in a terrorist group.

I have difficulties with this attempt at justification, while acknowledging that this effectively rules certain situations as being out of bounds for research. Perhaps this should be approached on a case by case basis, with exhaustive analysis of the ethical issues. However, I suggest that your own ethical dilemma is solved by recognizing that a situation, so sensitive that you need to be covert, is not one for the novice researcher.

It is still possible to take a full role as group member after making it clear from the outset that part of the reason for your involvement is the research. They will, of course, have to accept you on this basis and give their informed consent to the research (see chapter 5, p. 100). It is always possible that your presence will, in one or more ways, affect what is going on. This reactivity is a particular difficulty in participant observation. Logically, it isn't possible to have a definitive answer on your effect, as it would need you to observe when you weren't there! However, there are ways of reducing likely effects, such as prolonged involvement in the working of the group.

More marginal roles are possible. You might, as it were, 'take a back seat', not taking a prominent role when there is action, or have your role agreed as being the researcher in their midst.

Coming 'new' to a situation can pose difficult problems. You may feel that virtually nothing is going on, or that there is a confusing complexity. The jargon used, and local ways of doing things, may be very excluding. Traditional ethnographers take years to come to terms with what is happening. You have weeks or months at best. One possibility is to choose situations where you already have some familiarity and experience. A practitioner-researcher will have helpful previous experience, but making the transition from the practitioner role to participant observer with a research role has its own difficulties.

For participant observers, the data are typically written or taped accounts of what has been observed, made as soon as possible after the event. You may need to show considerable ingenuity to do this as unobtrusively as possible (nipping outside, or hiding in an empty room or wherever). Certainly it is a good rule to get as full an account as possible in the bag, before going to sleep each day. There is nothing to stop you supplementing accounts of what you have observed by informal interviews, getting copies of documents, etc.

Box 4.5 lists some of the advantages and disadvantages of using participant observation.

Observation can also be unstructured and non-participant, although this is relatively rare. This style can be used when it is desired to use unstructured qualitative approaches, but participation is not feasible or it is considered important to avoid reactivity, i.e. to avoid influencing or changing the observed situation. An example might be when studying crowd behaviour at a soccer match. Where, incidentally, the presence of high definition CCTV cameras to monitor troublemakers provides an opportunity to get hold of useful records for analysis – providing you can persuade security to release the tapes to you for this purpose. Such direct unobtrusive observation is one situation where it is generally accepted that informed consent from those videoed is not normally necessary. However, there are still ethical issues. Suppose you are making a video record of behaviour in a public park and capture a crime being committed. Do you report this to the police? My view would be that it depends – on the nature and seriousness of the crime, and on the situation. If you were doing this type of study (whether using a structured observation schedule or unstructured observation) you should have given prior consideration to likely scenarios in discussions with your supervisor, and should take further supervisor advice before acting.

Using observation in your project

If you are going to use observation as a data collection method, you are recommended to follow up one or more of the further reading texts below to get a detailed understanding of what is involved. The website gives links to other relevant websites.

Box 4.5 Some advantages and disadvantages of using participant observation

Advantages

1 It can be used to observe and analyse a very wide range of situations.
2 There is little or no need for equipment or prior preparation.
3 It provides the possibility of adopting a wide range of different participant roles (ranging from full participant through to marginal participant) depending on what is appropriate for the research, and which you feel most comfortable with.
4 It is capable of generating rich qualitative data. It is claimed that participant observation provides an opportunity to understand complex realities and relationships.
5 Extended involvement in a setting is likely to reduce any effects that the researcher might have on the situation.

Disadvantages

1 It can be very time-consuming and emotionally demanding.
2 There can be a problem finding opportunities to record what you have observed while it is fresh in your mind.
3 There is a danger of 'going native', with your research role being prejudiced by your involvement with the group and its values.
4 It can be hazardous for the researcher, not only in terms of physical safety, but also in being exposed to psychological and possibly legal risks, as well as ethical dilemmas.
5 The data can be overwhelming in both quantity and richness, hence difficult to analyse and interpret.

Further reading

De Walt, K. M. and De Walt, B. R. (2001) *Participant Observation: A guide for fieldworkers*. Lanham, MD: Altamira. Covers theoretical and historical background, but main focus is on practical applications and acquiring the techniques of participant observation.

Martin, P. and Bateson, P. (1993) *Measuring Behaviour: An introductory guide*. 2nd edition. Cambridge: Cambridge University Press. Very clear and concise, but with good coverage of what is involved in using structured observation.

Simpson, M. and Tuson, J. (2003) *Using Observation in Small-scale Research: A beginner's guide*. 2nd edition. Glasgow: The SCRE Centre. Short and very practical. Covers a range of approaches. Addressed to teachers but generally relevant.

Using Documents and Other Secondary Sources

Note: Documentary analysis was discussed in chapter 2 (p. 27) as an overall approach to social research. However, it is commonly used as an additional data collection method in a project using a different main data collection method.

The methods discussed so far in this chapter all involve you, as researcher, actively collecting the data. Data collected in this way are sometimes referred to as primary data. However, there is also the possibility of using, as sources of data, material that already exists, which is referred to as secondary data. Fields such as history and literature rely heavily on texts from the historical period being researched or the writer being studied. Generally, in almost all fields of research, there are existing documents that can be studied and analysed as data sources. These include such things as personal and business correspondence, archives containing the official proceedings of organizations, newspapers and magazines, biographies and autobiographies – to name but a few. A diary can be primary data when completed at the request of the researcher, usually to a specific format (see above, p. 80). Other diaries provide secondary data and can give a vivid first-hand account of the diarist's life (Pepys' seventeenth-century diaries being the classic example).

The term 'document' can encompass non-text material such as photographs, films and videos. Some draw it wider to include anything that a human being has produced or affected, which brings in works of art, architecture and design, and archaeological remains.

Somewhat confusingly, documents are, in some fields, referred to as primary sources. This is to distinguish them from secondary sources that are research reports such as journal articles or monographs.

There are also tertiary sources, which are articles and books which review secondary sources and are an invaluable way of getting a feel for what is known about a particular area. As all research calls for you to analyse such secondary and tertiary sources, the issues dealt with in the rest of this section are relevant, even if you decide not to employ documentary analysis of primary sources in your study.

Documentary analysis has major advantages and disadvantages, summarized in Box 4.6. The main advantages are that, with a little effort, you are almost certain to come across one or more relevant documents to analyse, and that it is usually a relatively low cost method in terms of the effort needed to acquire the documents. The main disadvantage arises from the document necessarily having been produced for some purpose other than to form part of your research. This means that it may well be silent on the particular topics that you are most interested in and, perhaps most importantly, that there are likely to be biases arising from the actual purpose for which the document was originally produced.

Box 4.6 Some advantages and disadvantages of using documentary analysis as a data collection method

Advantages

1 It is usually not difficult to get hold of relevant documents for little or no cost, particularly if you have access to the facilities of an academic library.
2 It is typically a cheap (in resource terms) means of generating substantial amounts of data.
3 It is amenable to a wide variety of qualitative and quantitative styles of analysis.
4 Documents are usually in a permanent form and can be returned to for re-analysis, or for the purposes of reliability checking.
5 It provides a potential subsidiary data collection method for almost all projects.

Disadvantages

1 As the document has been produced for a purpose other than for your research, you need to assess the extent to which this purpose is likely to affect the document.
2 Assessing the credibility of a document can be complex and difficult. Its authenticity or genuineness has to be established. As well as purpose, aspects such as the position, background, likely biases and prejudices of the author(s) have to be considered.
3 In contrast to the directness of observation, data from documentary analysis are at least two removes from reality. They are based on both the author(s) interpretation and on your own interpretation of this.

Note: Documentary analysis is treated in this text as a data collection method, but it is also an overall style or approach (see chapter 2, p. 27).

Because of this problem, it is advisable to combine documentary analysis with one or more additional data collection methods, such as interviews or some form of direct observation, whenever this is feasible. If you have to rely solely on documents, as in historical research or any form of research into past events, then possible bias has to be addressed by considering internal evidence as discussed below, and by comparing the messages given by a range of different documents.

Scott (1990) puts forward four criteria for assessing the quality of the data from documents; authenticity, credibility, representativeness and meaning.

Authenticity Is the document genuine or a fake? With historical documents, technical analysis of the paper, ink, and printing or writing used is carried out. For more modern documents, internal evidence is sought on matters such as inconsistencies of style, content or handwriting, on whether it comes from a suspect source, or has perhaps been in the hands of someone with a particular vested interest in its contents. However, even a document that lacks authenticity in some way may be of research value. Can you get evidence on why it was faked or tampered with?

Credibility This is whether it can be believed as not being biased or distorted. What can we find out about the person or group who produced the document and the purpose for which it was produced? Does it check with other sources of evidence and, if there are differences, can we link them to the reason why the document was produced?

Representativeness Does this appear to be a typical document? Or an unusual, atypical one? Both can be of value.

Meaning What does the document tell us? Generally, to understand this we need to have an appreciation of the context in which the document was produced (also called for when assessing credibility).

Library research

A project based exclusively on the analysis of documentary evidence is sometimes referred to as 'library research', although this becomes something of a misnomer when documents are increasingly available from the comfort of your own home through the internet. Some fields of study specifically exclude this type of solely document-based research and require you to collect primary data for yourself. In other fields it is the norm, but there may be a requirement that the study include analysis of primary sources (as defined above). Alternatively, analysis of existing journal articles or other accounts of research (i.e. secondary sources) might be acceptable, even perhaps a study reviewing reviews (i.e. based on tertiary sources). The basic rule – find out the rules for your project before committing yourself to a specific type of study.

The stance taken in this text is not to rule out any approach, providing that it satisfies the 'concern for truth' criterion introduced in chapter 2 (p. 18), and that it provides answers to a non-trivial set of research questions. While much of the text covers issues arising in and from the collection of primary data, the general approach is equally relevant to library, document-based research.

Unobtrusive measures

Documents are an example of a very particular type of 'trace' that people leave behind them. There are many others: hypodermic syringes left in public spaces, usage patterns of books and magazines in libraries, numbers of 'hits' on websites, etc. Use of these so-called 'unobtrusive measures' is regarded by many as a somewhat quirky method of collecting data but, with a little ingenuity, you might be able to come up with some low-cost additional data for your project. The text by Webb et al., in the further reading below, is a reprint of the classic text in this area and has many fascinating examples.

Using documents in your project

If you are going to use documentary analysis (or other unobtrusive measures) as a data collection method, you are recommended to follow up one or more of the further reading texts below to get a detailed understanding of what is involved. The website gives links to other relevant websites.

Further reading

Bonacci, M. A., Staines, G. M. and Johnson, K. (2000) *Social Sciences Research: Writing strategies for students.* Lanham, MD: Scarecrow Press. Covers all aspects of library research.

Hodson, R. (1999) *Analyzing Documentary Accounts.* London and Thousand Oaks, CA: Sage. Main focus is on the analysis of existing ethnographic material. Covers both quantitative and qualitative approaches.

Lee, R. M. (2000) *Unobtrusive Measures in Social Research.* Maidenhead, Berks: Open University Press. More accessible than the Webb et al. text.

McCulloch, G. (2004) *Documentary Research: In education, history and the social sciences.* London: Routledge Falmer. Explores the uses of a wide range of documentary source material including visual sources. Covers their use in combination with other methods.

Scott, J. (1990) *A Matter of Record: Documentary sources in social research.* Cambridge: Polity. Good reference text for those beginning research using documentary methods.

Webb, E. J., Campbell, D. T., and Swartz, R. D. (2000) *Unobtrusive Measures.* London and Thousand Oaks, CA: Sage. Reprint of classic text first published in 1965. Second edition (1981) has additional examples.

Other Methods

The preceding sections by no means exhaust the possible methods of data collection that you might consider. Some research, particularly experimental studies, calls for a one-off approach where the method flows directly from the specific research questions. Many of the more specialized techniques that you may come across, or be recommended to use (for example, discourse analysis – the detailed analysis of conversations or other language samples), call for substantial training and experience. Others, for example the use of repertory grids, are set in a particular theoretical perspective and risk misuse when just seen as a technique for collecting data. Robson (2002; pp. 362–70) covers a range of additional methods which you might consider if still searching.

However, my advice would be to stick with the mainstream methods already covered in the chapter. None of them is beyond the reach of the first-time researcher, although your preparatory pilot work may be as much to help you achieve confidence with using the technique as anything else.

Note: Several of the methods discussed in the chapter are amenable to use in an online version. Questionnaires and interviews are now increasingly used in this way. For example, rather than using the post or telephone, an e-mail is sent to participants who respond by e-mail. The website gives examples.

Using Multiple Methods

Remember that you don't have to restrict yourself to a single data collection method. For example, interviewing can often be used alongside other methods. Complementing survey results with interviews, or using group interviews as part of pilot work prior to using a second method, are just two of several possibilities. More generally, keep open the possibility of using different methods for the different phases of the project.

The main disadvantage is that using more than one method inevitably takes more time and effort, but this has to be balanced against the wider perspective gained. A sensible strategy when, as is usually the case, you are short of time, is to have one main data collection method. Then to support this with a second method that is low-cost in terms of the efforts you have to make (e.g. use of short relatively informal interviews, or analysis of documents you have acquired, or completion of a short questionnaire). Up to 10 per cent of your time on this subsidiary method can be profitable.

Which Method?

The choice of the main method of data collection for your project is multiply determined. Have you got the necessary skills to use the method or can you acquire them in time? Would you feel comfortable using the method? Can you see yourself actually carrying out a participant observation study? How do you feel about administering possibly intrusive tests to people? Such concerns limit your selection of a method.

As with the choice of topic, of main research question(s) and of the overall style or approach of the study, the method of data collection may appear self-evident. If you are following a topic suggested by a supervisor where there is previous research, this may well include suggestions about method. With topics and research questions you have sorted out for yourself, the sources of previous work that you have discovered will again suggest, not only the general approach but also the main method that might be used. However, don't feel totally constrained by past practice. It is safer to follow in others' footsteps, but it is interesting to ask yourself 'could this be approached differently?'.

Your choice of the overall approach to the project gives pointers to possible methods as indicated in Box 4.7. Don't regard these as set in stone.

As discussed in chapter 3, p. 51, the main research questions provide an important basis for the choice of approach. Revisiting them helps to decide on the most appropriate data collection methods, particularly in case study and evaluation research designs.

Box 4.7 Data collection methods used in different approaches

Style or approach of the project	Likely main data collection method(s)	Possible secondary data collection method(s)
Action research	Interviews, participant observation	Documentary analysis
Case study	Multiple (often includes interviews, observation and documentary analysis)	
Evaluation research	Any (depends on purpose of evaluation)	Documentary analysis
Experimental approach	Typically specially designed instrument (often structured observation, questionnaire or test)	Informal interviews
Qualitative (ethnographic)	Participant observation	Documentary analysis, interviews
Qualitative (grounded theory)	Interviews, participant observation	Documentary analysis
Survey approach	Structured questionnaires or interviews, possibly structured observation	Informal interviews

Further Reading

Bryman, A. (2004) *Social Research Methods*. 2nd edition. Oxford: Oxford University Press.

Cohen, L., Manion, L. and Morrison, K. (2000) *Research Methods in Education*. 5th edition. London: Routledge Falmer.

Hoyle, R. H., Judd, C. M. and Harris, M. J. (2001) *Research Methods in Social Relations*. 7th edition. Belmont, CA: Wadsworth.

Robson, C. (2002) *Real World Research: A resource for social scientists and practitioner-researchers*. 2nd edition. Oxford: Blackwell.

Sarantakos, S. (2004) *Social Research*. 3rd edition. Basingstoke, Hants: Palgrave Macmillan.

This is a selection of five 'big' research methods texts, useful if you want more details of particular methods (or on assessing reliability and validity). They are likely to be found in many academic libraries – earlier editions are worth consulting if the latest one is not available.

Silverman, D. (2004) *Doing Qualitative Research: A practical handbook*. 2nd edition. London and Thousand Oaks, CA: Sage. Excellent chapter on reliability and validity in flexible design projects.

See also the suggestions for further reading on specific methods of data collection which are provided after discussion of that method.

Chapter 4 Tasks

Review the (provisional) decisions you made for the chapter 3 tasks. Modify any that you have had second thoughts about. In the light of these decisions:

1 *Decide on the main data collection method.* For most undergraduate projects, a single main data collection method is as much as you can cope with given the time and resources available. The main exception is the case study where you need two or more to get the most out of the approach.

2 *Decide on a secondary data collection method* (not essential but can be very helpful). Choose something cheap and straightforward, such as short informal interviews. Don't plan to spend more than a small fraction of the time of your data-gathering exercise on this secondary method.

3 *Consider how the data are to be analysed.* Now that you have sorted out the design of your project and the data collection method(s), you are in a position to think about ways in which the data might be analysed. Refer to projects and journal articles using similar designs and methods for ideas. *Seek advice from your supervisor and/or someone with a background in data analysis.*

Part II

Doing It

Sooner or later you are going to have to get down to collecting some data. Making the transition from preparation mode to action mode can be difficult for some. Some people persuade themselves that they're not quite ready and need to do more reading, or that they should think it over some more before committing themselves. Others are itching to get on with the real work and skimp on the preparation.

As discussed in chapter 2, p. 22, fixed and flexible designs differ considerably in the degree of preparedness needed before you start on the main data collection exercise. With a fixed design, such as in survey or experimental research, meticulous pre-planning is essential. Part of this pre-planning is piloting so that you can have confidence that what you are proposing is likely to be feasible. In flexible design studies, such as most qualitative research, it is neither possible nor desirable to get things tied down in advance to the same extent. You still need to have a broad focus or area of interest and some idea of where you are going both literally (knowing the situation or site you will be involved with) and conceptually (having an initial, probably tentative and fluid, set of research questions). However, a central feature of flexible design research is that you allow things to evolve. How you proceed depends to a considerable extent on how things go. You follow up promising leads. Abandon blind alleys. Develop and refine your research question(s) as you appreciate more what is going on and how it might be understood.

5

Practicalities of Data Collection

Once you have chosen the method(s) appropriate to the project, this, together with the decisions already made about research questions and the general style or approach you are going to adopt, puts in place the main building blocks of the project design. There are, of course, many detailed decisions to be made in preparing for, and running, the project. These include the 'who', 'what', 'where', and 'when' questions ('why' has already been addressed when considering the purpose of the project – to explore, explain or whatever, see chapter 2, p. 19):

☐ *Who?* Which participants, and how many, are you going to select?
☐ *What and where?* Which settings should you choose for data collection? What kinds of setting and where geographically (and, again, how many)?
☐ *When?* What date do you start, and how long do you go on for?

Many of these questions may have pretty self-evident answers. The place where you collect data may be determined by the nature of the project. There may only be, say, a couple of weeks when the data have to be collected. There will usually be some freedom in who, and how many, you ask to participate. This is a sampling issue and is discussed in the following section.

In fixed designs, you run pilot studies which will, among other things, help you assess whether your plan is realistic. In flexible designs, you have to keep a continuing watching brief while collecting data. Can you afford to spend more time on promising aspects? Can you curtail aspects when time is short? Practicalities of this kind are discussed in the following sections.

Sampling and Sample Sizes

The 'who', 'what', 'where' and 'when' questions are essentially about sampling. You can't do everything so you have to be selective. In particular, limits have to be set on the number of participants you get involved with. In other words, you must select a sample of participants.

As discussed in chapter 2, p. 41, some types of social research, notably the survey, rely heavily on this sample being representative of some wider population. If this is the case, it is then possible to make statistical generalizations about aspects of the population from what you find out in your study about the sample. These are always estimates, but it is possible to assess the likely degree of error in such estimates. Such surveys – usually called sample surveys – are widespread, not only in research but also in political polling and marketing. Their design and analysis can be sophisticated. In applied fields, there are commercial implications of getting inaccurate results which help ensure that they get it right.

Representative samples

Suppose that you are carrying out a survey of student satisfaction in your college. The relevant population might be all those enrolled on courses on a particular date. A representative sample, where one can legitimately make generalizations from what one finds in the sample of students participating in your survey to the population of students in the college as a whole, would have to ensure that all enrolled students would have the same chance of being included in the sample. This is not an easy task.

The most straightforward way, conceptually, is to go for a simple random sample. To do this, you need a list of all students enrolled on the date that you have chosen (this list is called the sampling frame). Say that you decide on a 10 per cent sample (see the discussion below on sample sizes). The traditional way of selecting the sample was to use some type of lottery approach (e.g. slips of paper each with a number representing a student on the list) or random number tables, where selections are made until you have your sample. 'Research Randomizer' (www.randomizer.org/) is a website which provides a very easy-to-use way of performing random sampling and is highly recommended. Follow their tutorial if in doubt.

Armed with your sample list of names (from their number codes), you proceed to contact them by post, e-mail or whatever means you have decided. At this stage, you will encounter problems in getting hold of some of them – perhaps they have left, or there is a mistake in the list or whatever. It is advisable to select any necessary replacements in the same way that the original sample was selected. See the suggested further reading for the tactics to deal with these, and other, complexities.

A simple random sample of all students may not be the best way of approaching the selection of a sample. Perhaps your main interest is in students following a first degree course. If so you can simplify your task by making students on such courses your population. Suppose that you want to ensure that your sample includes reasonable numbers from each of the schools or departments in the university. Or from all courses. Or to make sure that the sample has the same proportion of male and female students as there are overall. It is feasible to cover issues like this by more complex sampling procedures, including cluster and stratified sampling (see the further reading).

Non-probability samples

Small-scale research projects often do not attempt to use the ways of obtaining representative samples discussed above. Convenience samples are common. Researchers grab hold of whoever they can; friends, relatives, fellow-students, passers-by, etc. There is nothing necessarily wrong or inappropriate in doing this, provided you make clear in your report what has been done, and provided that you do not claim that your findings are statistically generalizable in the way that random samples are. Experimental designs often use convenience samples. They rely on random assignment of participants to the different experimental conditions, which enables valid comparisons to be made between the conditions but still leaves their generalizability problematic.

Flexible design research projects, particularly when following a grounded theory approach, commonly make use of purposive samples. Here, there is a deliberate attempt to select participants with known characteristics. These might include persons likely to be particularly knowledgeable, influential or otherwise key to understanding the situation. Then 'theoretical sampling' can be a principle of selection of those who will help in testing out or further understanding the emerging theory.

In situations where it is difficult to get hold of participants, perhaps because the topic is sensitive, snowball sampling can be used. Having got hold of one relevant person and, say, interviewed them, you ask if they know of others who could be interviewed on the topic. And so on . . .

Market researchers and political pollsters often use quota samples. This approach depends on a knowledge of the characteristics of the population of interest – perhaps the relative proportions of persons in different socio-economic groupings, gender ratios, etc. The researcher's task is to get hold of quotas with different characteristics. If done conscientiously, this produces samples which are representative of the number of those with specific characteristics in the population. A similar approach uses telephone surveys where the results are weighted to correspond to the proportions in the population. Quota samples do not produce fully representative samples in the way that random sampling does. Trawling the high street some afternoon to get your quota of manual labourers, professionals, etc., won't necessarily give you a truly representative picture of the population as a whole.

Informed Consent

The principle of informed consent is sacrosanct (see the discussion on ethics in chapter 3, p. 64). Participants* should know what they are letting themselves in for and give explicit agreement to this. Whether or not a formal consent form should be used depends on the particular circumstances of the study and should be discussed and agreed with your supervisor. Indications favouring the use of formal consent forms include the possibility of stress or distress to those taking part. Some areas, such as social psychology, have made substantial use of deception in the past – the true purpose of the study is not revealed and a cover story used. The justification for such practices has been that, if informed of the true purpose, participants would have behaved differently in some way. Deception is still used by reputable researchers but you are advised not to use it unless it is explicitly sanctioned by your supervisor (and an ethics committee). If deception is used, participants should be debriefed as to the true purpose of the study afterwards. Establishing whether some of those involved saw through the deception can provide you with useful information.

Laboratory Research

The practicalities of collecting data are very different for those working in a laboratory and those who have to leave the familiar environment of their college and enter what social researchers call 'the field'. If you are carrying out your research in some type of laboratory, this is, as it were, a home fixture. A major task is to persuade possible participants to enter your territory through flattery, bribery, appealing to their altruism or by whatever ethical means are at your disposal.

Gaining Access for Field Research

Research outside the laboratory is an away fixture, out in the big wide world. In this situation, gaining access can be a problem. The difficulty varies widely from setting to setting and appears to be getting more problematic. Worries about paedophiles can make studies involving the observation of children sen-

---

* Some disciplines, particularly those such as experimental psychology where most research is laboratory based, have traditionally referred to those taking part in their research studies as 'subjects'. The term is now generally recognized as having unfortunate connotations, with the suggestion that people are being 'subjected' to something that may not be very pleasant. It has largely been replaced by the more neutral 'participant'. The website gives links covering the issue.

sitive. The management of commercial centres such as shopping malls are likely to be wary of anyone pestering their customers and getting in the way of them buying things.

Just as you can take it as a good working assumption that all research involving people has ethical implications (chapter 3, p. 64), the basic rule is that you need formal permission to carry out your research study in any private setting or any public setting where there is not totally open access (e.g. schools or hospitals). Again, as with ethical considerations, if you are a student you should receive advice and support from your supervisor. In any case, a formal letter setting out what you are hoping to do, and the kind of access you are asking for, is highly desirable. Similarly, you should receive a formal note in response agreeing to the access (if you don't get one, you or your supervisor will have to follow it up).

In practice, personal face-to-face contact is more likely to get a result, but it is also important to get things in writing. If anything goes wrong, this can be a valuable safeguard. It's not unknown for a manager to try to wriggle out of a tricky situation by claiming that you were doing something that wasn't previously agreed.

On a more positive note, establishing a link when seeking access may lead to the person being interested in what you are doing and facilitating your involvement. It may even be that through discussion you can refocus your study to cover aspects that the firm or organization would find of direct value. If this is the case, they will be keen to facilitate your work.

More generally, you should beware of just using the organization, or other setting which is letting you have access, as 'research-fodder'. They could legitimately feel that they were being used just to help you get an award. This feeling could inoculate them from any further involvement with research. Your aim should be to leave them at least as favourably disposed to research as when you started – preferably more so. The discussion of surveys in chapter 2 (p. 41) warned about 'questionnaire fatigue'. This is an example of the more general phenomenon of 'research fatigue'. Some groups (for example refugee community organizations) get barraged with requests from researchers and consequently may be reluctant to participate. You have to be sensitive to these issues and respect such feelings, and to be prepared to change the focus of your project; no participants, no project!

A good rule is that participants should get something out of the experience. At a minimum this should be an offer by you to let them see your report, preferably in a form which is written to communicate to them (which is not necessarily the same format as the report needed for your course). This is something that could be written into any contract you enter into with your hosts (see following section). In some situations, it may be appropriate for you to agree to provide recommendations for improvement or change. You could also offer to give a presentation to those who have taken part in your research. People often have considerable interest in the views of an outsider such as yourself into what is going on.

The process of obtaining formal approval can take a long time. You need to find the right person, or persons, to contact. Your supervisor should have experience of this and be able to give you help. Avoid just writing 'cold' without prior informal contact. Your letter could sit in someone's in-tray before being binned or it could do a tour around the organization with nobody viewing it as their responsibility. Doing research in some settings will require clearance by a body outside the actual place in which you hope to work. Perhaps police checks are required to establish that you don't have a criminal record, which can take months. The message is that, as soon as it becomes clear that you would like to carry out the research in a particular setting and you know the broad outlines of what you propose to do, start the process of gaining access. Don't wait until you have completed all your preparation and want to start the next week.

Clearing the hurdle of formal approval doesn't necessarily mean that you are going to be welcomed in the organization, classroom, ward, shop-floor or wherever. The people who you hope will participate may be suspicious of you and of your motives. If there is a history of bad relations with management, or they are under stress or facing threats of change or closure, you are unlikely to get co-operation. You may well be viewed as a management stooge. If your study has, or might appear to have, an evaluative dimension (see chapter 2, p. 32), word is likely to get out that you are evaluating their performance in some way, with the possibility of dire consequences for them – and for your relationship.

It is important that you find ways of getting over to all those likely to be involved what you are doing and why. And, of course, that your motives are pure and there is no hidden agenda (see discussion on ethics, chapter 3, p. 64). One strategy is to establish a relationship of trust with an influential and popular person in the organization, who will effectively act as your informal sponsor ('She's all right. We can trust her'). This calls for a certain amount of understanding of the dynamics within the setting, which may take time for you to develop. It is not unknown for someone who occupies a marginal or isolated position to want to chum up with the researcher. This can have the effect of you sharing their marginal or isolated position.

The default position is that everyone involved should have given their informed consent to taking part. However, use your common sense. In a study of purchasing patterns in a supermarket, the extent to which you seek informed consent will depend on the exact nature of the study. You don't need consent from shoppers whom you simply observe, possibly through closed circuit TV. If, on the other hand, you interview shoppers about their purchases, they should agree to take part knowing what you are doing, and with an assurance of confidentiality.

Formal and informal contracts

There is much to be said for preparing and agreeing a formal contract with whoever is the responsible person in the organization. It should specify both the nature of your research and the access conditions. There will also be agreements about confidentiality and people's rights with respect to any report that is produced. Try to get the agreement worded so that they have the right to see and comment on drafts, and possibly add their own comments, but that they can't veto the production of a report. See the website for relevant links.

Such written agreements are valuable in case something goes wrong, or personnel change. If, when you approach the organization, they suggest that it is all fine and they don't want to bother with a formal contract, it is advisable to send them a letter specifying your understanding of what they have agreed to (perhaps with a note saying that if you haven't heard from them by . . ., you will take it that they agree, and that you look forward to seeing them on Monday next).

Organizations with little or no previous experience of research can be problematic. They may have exaggerated views of the benefits you will provide, or expect to be able to dictate what you do. In any organization the gate-keepers (i.e. whoever can control your access) may want to set unreasonable constraints on the project. These issues have to be talked through so that there is mutual understanding and you end up with a situation with which you, and your supervisor, feel you can cope with.

Getting on and getting out

Getting on in the place where you are doing your project can be very straightforward, or almost impossible, and anywhere in between. There is no rule against enjoying yourself, providing this doesn't get in the way of your research role. If you land in a situation that you find stressful, you need help. You can, for example, find yourself torn between groups with different interests who seek to recruit you to their view of problems or difficulties. Your support network should be in place before you get into the research situation. This can be your supervisor at the end of a phone line, or available for texting or e-mailing, or a colleague or group of colleagues with whom you can have informal discussion sessions either via the Web or face-to-face (see chapter 1, p. 11, on support groups).

Suppose that you come across a situation where you suspect, or are told, that something illegal or unethical is taking place. Perhaps there is some fiddle going on where employees are falsifying expense accounts, or so-called care staff are mistreating confused old people in a residential home. This is where you definitely need advice and support. You must discuss this with your supervisor, who should advise you about the appropriate action to be taken – and about who should take the action (see section on ethics in chapter 3, p. 64).

As a novice researcher, you should not be carrying out your research in a situation where there appears to be a chance that your safety, or health, is at risk. Possible risks include:

☐ the risk of physical threat or abuse
☐ the risk of psychological trauma or consequences as a result of actual or threatened violence or the nature of what is disclosed during the research
☐ the risk of being in a compromising situation in which there might be accusations of improper behaviour
☐ increased exposure to general risks of everyday life and social interaction: travel, infectious illness and accident.

Craig et al. (2000), from which the above points have been taken, provide an excellent review of researcher safety interests (see also website). Again, this is an issue to be talked through with your supervisor.

Just as it can be difficult to make the transition between preparation for the project and data collection, it can be hard to extricate yourself from the research setting. You can usually persuade yourself that staying on for a bit longer will yield valuable data. And anyway the task of analysing and interpreting the data and writing the report can appear aversive. Usually, harsh practicalities take over. If you don't leave now, you will never complete by the deadline when reports have to be submitted.

This is best handled by deciding, before you start the main data collection, the date that you must pull out by. Make this part of your formal or informal contract with participants, and make sure that everyone knows this. Often it can be valuable to factor in a return visit at a date close to the time by which you have to complete. The visit can be used for feedback to those concerned (although, if pushed, this could be at a later date after the deadline). It may also give you additional information on how things have changed or developed since you left and perhaps give you the opportunity to try out with participants some of your findings and interpretations.

Insider research

Insider research is research carried out by someone who, prior to the research, has already got some role or position in the setting or organization that is the focus of the research. For an undergraduate research project, this would be most likely to be carried out by a practitioner, such as a teacher or social worker, currently following a degree programme whether on a full-time or part-time basis. Focusing the project on your work setting has several attractions. You will have both formal and informal knowledge about the place where you work, helping you to avoid pitfalls that an outsider might not. In some cases, it is an explicit requirement, or at least an expectation, that you will carry out something likely to be of value to the service that is supporting your involvement with the course. Having done a project that is seen as valuable by colleagues and managers will stand you in good stead in your future career.

Other possibilities include linking the project to an involvement you have with, say, church or youth work, sports or athletics clubs, choirs, orchestras and student union activities, including support services. A former student of mine was a keen surfer and set up a project on 'surf bunnies', female members of her surfing group. Unfortunately the lure of the surf proved too strong and her project was never completed, which is one danger of following up something you are keenly interested in.

While insider research has many attractions, it has its difficulties. The fact that you already have some role in the setting, distinct from that of researcher, will cause complications. Interviewing colleagues can be fraught with status issues. If you have a relatively lowly position then managers may not be forthcoming. If high, then the workers will watch what they say.

Insider research seems particularly prone to raising ethical issues. Suppose that you hear or discover something with your researcher hat on which reveals questionable practices. You should seek to anticipate likely problems and to have made it clear to participants that, while you will normally respect confidentiality, there are limits in relation to acts such as client abuse and other clearly illegal activities. Again, as discussed earlier, you should expect to receive advice and support on any such matters from your supervisor and the support networks of colleagues.

Pilots

In fixed design research, such as experiments and surveys, piloting is a crucial part of the process. Ideally, this style of research calls for the main data collection exercise to go like clockwork. You have a detailed plan worked out in advance and the task is to put that plan into operation. Admittedly, we don't live in an ideal world, and things may crop up that force you to modify your plans (the most common scenario being that you realize you won't be able to do everything you planned to – which is why you should give some thought to a Plan B – a 'traded down' design which will at least give you something to analyse and discuss – see below; p. 107).

Running pilot studies is the main way of reality-testing your proposals and fine tuning your plan. This involves trying out all aspects of the data collection on a small-scale. The specific details vary from one project to another but typically you pilot using a small sample selected in the same way as proposed for the main exercise. You have to ensure that the main exercise won't be contaminated by your pilot work (e.g. so that you're not in danger of selecting some of the same participants; or that details aren't passed on from those in the pilot to later participants). Pre-testing of all procedures should take place in the pilot work. Are there problems in understanding questions or instructions? Are tasks too easy or too difficult? Debriefing of pilot participants, to find out any problems or issues from their perspective, can be very illuminating.

Pilot work should extend, beyond data collection aspects, to piloting what you plan to do with the data subsequently. It can be helpful to use the pilot data as a basis for generating some dummy data from a similar number of participants to those you expect to have in the main data collection exercise. You then use this data to test out whether you know what to do to carry out your proposed basic data analyses.

If the pilot work throws up problems, these have to be addressed before you proceed. If these are major – say, several of the pilot participants misunderstand instructions – then, if at all possible, do some further pilot work before moving to the main data collection.

Flexible design research is more forgiving. The details of what you are doing in say, a case study, can and should be sorted out as you feel your way through, gaining access and establishing trust with those involved. A rather different form of piloting may well be needed if you are a novice researcher. Some prior development of the researcher skills that the project calls for will help you feel more confident when interacting with participants. For example, some sessions of participant observation in settings similar to the one in your project can be confidence boosting.

Collecting the Data

Your pilot work should have given you the chance of testing out the way you are going about the task of data collection. Obviously, the specific details of this task vary from one data collection method to another but the general question you should ask yourself is 'What is the simplest and easiest way that I can collect the data that I need to get answers to the research questions?' Just because you have the possibility of, say, videotaping sessions, doesn't mean that you necessarily have to do so. I recall, to my shame, having a large cupboard full of video cassettes from one project which we never got round to analysing. They were collected because it seemed a good idea at the time, without our costing out the time and effort needed to transcribe them with a deadline looming.

Incidentally, the videos were all destroyed a long time ago and the project was before the UK Data Protection Act 1988 came into force. Under the provisions of that Act it is very clear that you should not collect more data than is going to be used (see the section on ethics in chapter 3, p. 64).

For many projects, audio-taping is a preferred option, particularly when using semi-structured interviews. Work out in advance what you are going to do with them. Do you need to transcribe them all, or will it be sufficient to replay them and make notes, perhaps with selective transcription of relevant responses?

Whatever equipment you use, it is crucial you know how to operate it. If you are audio-taping, get hold of the best quality equipment you can find and make sure when piloting that the microphone picks up voices satisfactorily. Make sure that you have any necessary spares, particularly new fully charged batteries. Train yourself to keep an eye on when you get to the end of a tape so that you don't miss the last minutes of an interview.

You need a system. Prepare a list of what you need to do. Things like: phone John just before the visit you arranged; check any equipment is in working order before visit, spare batteries, etc.; bring supply of blank tapes; check equipment set up and working; label copies of data tapes, notes, files, etc. Sort this out when piloting, making sure you include everything important.

Remember that you need to time budget not only the actual data collection but also the time and resources required once you have the data. It doesn't make sense to have all this lovely data if you haven't got the time to get as much as you can out of it. The process of analysis and interpretation of the data is covered in the next chapter.

What to Do if You Run into Difficulties or out of Time

If the agreed departure date is looming, without your having completed all you had hoped and planned to do, a swift review of the situation is called for. It is important that you give yourself sufficient time not only to analyse and interpret the data that you do have but also to make the most of it in your report. What you don't do is to stick, willy-nilly, to the original data collection plan. There are no prizes for having reams of unanalysed data and no report.

It is highly advisable to have given some thought to a Plan B *before you get into this position*. That is a slimmed down version with, perhaps, fewer interviews or only studying one site rather than three, or whatever. Something which, barring an absolute disaster, you are confident you can complete. If you are in difficulty, focus on this slimmed down version and regard anything else you complete as a bonus which you might be able to stitch in somehow.

Lots of things can go wrong and some probably will. Participants may decide that they want out. People's personal circumstances change and they may not wish to continue. If a few withdraw, this shouldn't be a problem. In surveys, you should have a procedure for selecting replacements (see p. 98). In flexible designs, you can usually deal with this by finding someone else who is willing to help, though it can be a real problem if the person opting out is one of the key persons in the situation. If many people want to withdraw, then this is likely to be symptomatic of a serious problem which may be specific to the research or indicative of a wider malaise. Either way, seek advice from your supervisor. You might have to start again in another setting unless the root of the problem can be dealt with.

You may run into design difficulties. Perhaps you find that a randomization process, say, the random allocation of participants to experimental or control groups, hasn't worked properly. It's not unknown for someone you relied on to do this, deciding that it would be better if certain people were in the experimental group by fiddling the allocation. The moral is to keep such aspects under your control. However, if a design breakdown does occur, it may well be that you have to live with the situation. Providing that you give an honest account of what happened, and take into account the changed situation when analysing and interpreting the data, you should be able to rescue the situation.

Don't even despair about an absolute disaster. Unless it's your total incompetence or general lack of ability to organize (which I'm sure it isn't), something must have happened externally to lead to the disaster. With ingenuity, you ought to be able to make something of this. Remember, what you need to produce is a well written, professionally presented report which gives data-driven answers to a set of research questions. There is no iron rule that says these must be the questions you initially planned to answer. If the disaster has struck, you are, however, likely to be light on data. An account of your journey from initial to final questions is helpful not only in legitimately bulking up your report but also in demonstrating your ability to retrieve a difficult situation. It is far better to deal with this honestly and openly, rather than trying to hide, or gloss over, problems.

Further Reading

Henry, G. T. (1990) *Practical Sampling*. London and Thousand Oaks, CA: Sage. Short, clear and very useful if you have a sampling problem to sort out.

Howard, K., Sharp, J. A. and Peters, J. (2002) *The Management of a Student Research Project*. 3rd edition. Aldershot: Gower. Gives suggestions on what you need to consider to complete the project. Very useful if you have a complicated project and/or are not good at organization.

Knight, P. T. (2002) *Small-scale Research: Pragmatic inquiry in social science and the caring professions*. London and Thousand Oaks, CA: Sage. Section on 'doing it' (pp. 161–72) covers likely mishaps and a full range of other practical issues.

Chapter 5 Tasks

1 *Work out a project schedule* The schedule should include:

☐ a list of all the things you need to do up to and including handing in your completed project report
☐ the sequence in which they have to be done, and
☐ your estimate of the time each will take.

A good way of doing this is to draw a chart where each task takes up one row (see the examples on pp. 110–11). Tasks can run in sequence, in parallel or overlapping. Keep tasks to a manageable number (say up to 20) so you can fit the chart on a single page. The examples are just word-processed tables. Versions of the charts using horizontal bars with lengths corresponding to start and stop times of each activity are known as Gantt charts and can be produced using specialist software (see the website).

When you are actually collecting data you will need to:

☐ *Keep it up to date* Mark the chart as tasks are completed. If a task takes longer than anticipated, or starts late, revise the chart
☐ *Take emergency action* if it looks as if delays threaten you not being able to complete by the deadline (see 'What to do if you run into difficulties or out of time', p. 107).

2 *Work out a possible Plan B* What bits of your plan could you jettison in an emergency? What is the minimum in terms of sample size, number of settings visited, persons interviewed, amount of time in the setting, etc. which will give sufficient information to be able to get at least some kind of answer to your main research question?

Note: Return to complete this task when you have read the next two chapters and have a clearer idea of what is likely to be involved in analysing your data and writing the report.

Examples of project schedules

A fixed design project	Jun.	Jul.	Aug.	Sept.	Oct.	Nov.	Dec.	Jan.	Feb.	Mar.	Apr.	May
Deciding project focus	xx											
Design decisions (approach, methods, research questions)	==xx	xxxx		x===								
Reading, library and internet searching	xxxx	xxxx		xxx=				x===	xx==			
Ethics committee deadline				**14th**								
Negotiate access					xxx							
Write questionnaire				==xx								
Pilot questionnaire					xxx=							
Revise questionnaire					===x							
Main data collection						==xx	xxx=					
Data analysis								xxxx				
Write report sections (literature review: methodology; analysis)		=xx=							xxxx			
Write full draft report										xxxx	xxxx	
Seminar presentation											**14th**	
Draft to supervisor											**30th**	
Produce final draft												=xx
Completion deadline												**21st**

A flexible design project	Jun.	Jul.	Aug.	Sept.	Oct.	Nov.	Dec.	Jan.	Feb.	Mar.	Apr.	May
Deciding project focus	xx											
Design decisions (approach, methods, research questions)	==xx	xxxx		x===		==x=		==x=				
Reading, library and internet searching	xxxx	xxxx		xxx=		x		x====	xx===			
Ethics committee deadline				**14th**								
Negotiate access		==xx										
Data collection				==xx		==xx	xxx=		xx			
Data analysis				===x		===x	===xx	xxxx				
Write report sections (literature review: methodology; analysis)		==xx=				xx==			==xx			
Write full draft report										xxxx	xxxx	
Seminar presentation											**14th**	
Draft to supervisor											**30st**	
Produce final draft												==xx
Completion deadline												**21st**

Note:

Part III

Making Something of It

Collecting data almost inevitably depends on your getting active co-operation from others, usually the people participating in your interviews, filling in your questionnaires, etc. However, once you have that data, making something of it is very much up to you. This can come as a relief. It is something you can get stuck into, without having to rely on the vagaries of others.

But it is sensible to seek advice, particularly if you have substantial amounts of quantitative data, which might require statistical treatment. Or, for that matter, substantial amounts of qualitative data, when it may be helpful to use a software package for analysis. While all researchers, even first-time ones, are expected to carry out a competent analysis of their data, it is now widely accepted that the skill called for in this area is more that of knowing how to get advice from a data analysis expert, than being such an expert in your own right (however, as always, check what the expectations and regulations are for your course).

Recall also, that, as stressed in the tasks for chapter 4, p. 94, this is advice that you should have sought when finalizing the design of your study. It is an aspect of the so-called 'sod's law' (known in more polite circles as the 'law of maximum perversity') that, if you haven't considered how your data are to be analysed in advance of their collection, you end up with something that is an unanalysable mish-mash. Don't test the applicability of this law.

In fixed designs, the main data analysis takes place as a separate and distinctive phase after you have completed the main data collection exercise. If you have done prior piloting, it has already been pointed out that it is a good idea to do an earlier analysis of the results, partly to draw as many lessons as possible from the pilot, but also so that you can pilot the analysis itself (taking note that full analyses aren't necessary and are unlikely to be feasible because of the smaller numbers involved).

In flexible designs, analysis is much more intermingled with the data collection process. Some analysis of the initial data is needed to help guide later data collection. This does not preclude later and more extensive analysis, after the main data collection is completed.

Ideally, you should have built in a little leeway in your time-planning so that if something previously unexpected arises from the data analysis, there is some opportunity to return to the setting where you have been collecting data to check it out in some way.

6

Analysing and Interpreting Your Findings

All data analysis can also be considered as a process of interpretation, of dealing with the raw data in such ways that the messages contained in the data become clear. However, having done this to the best of your ability, you need to take an overview of what you have found. This overall interpretation forms the concluding section of the chapter.

What This Chapter Tries to Do

This chapter does not aim to provide comprehensive coverage of all aspects of data analysis. That would call for a much longer book solely devoted to the topic, as listed in the further reading section at the end of the chapter. It does seek to provide an introduction to important aspects of the analysis of both qualitative and quantitative analysis.

The section on quantitative analysis concentrates on simple ways of describing, summarizing and displaying numerical data. It makes no attempt (beyond giving references at the end of the chapter and material on the website) to cover complex statistical analyses that may be called for by those working in disciplines where such analyses are expected. However, my experience is that students in these fields not uncommonly make a poor job of the simpler aspects of data analysis. So, I hope that reminders will not come amiss.

For those without a strong statistical background I hope that you get the message that a perfectly adequate treatment of numerical data can often be achieved by simple summary statistics and clear displays. Even in projects with predominantly qualitative data, there are usually some numbers around which, simply but adequately dealt with, can enhance the overall analysis.

In somewhat similar manner, the treatment of qualitative data analysis makes no attempt to provide coverage of the many and varied approaches that are current (though, again there are references at the end of the chapter and relevant material on the website). Some general features of qualitative data analysis common to several specific approaches are summarized as an introduction to those unfamiliar with the field. This is followed by what is, I hope, sufficient coverage of the widely used grounded theory approach to enable you to assess whether or not it is appropriate for your project.

If your project is very largely quantitative, this section should provide pointers for the treatment of any qualitative data, including data from a second, subsidiary, data collection method.

Preparing for Analysis

The first step is to know, in some detail, exactly what data you have. The second is to make sure you have it in an easily accessible form. This is the stage when the systematic researcher comes into their own and the disorganized one suffers.

With fixed designs, you will have decided at the design stage what data you are going to collect so you should know what to expect. The decision about the main way in which you are going to analyse these data should also have been made then. If things haven't worked out quite as you anticipated, say, if one or more of the sites where you were going to collect data pulls out at a late stage, which forces changes, then you are going to have to do the best with the data you have. Don't worry. You can almost always make something of partial data.

If you have followed the advice in chapter 4 and devoted a little time and effort to using a second, subsidiary type of data collection, the results from this can be dealt with in a more open-ended manner. Essentially, you explore what you have got and see if it helps throw light on the findings from your main data analysis.

With flexible designs, you won't know in advance exactly what data, either in amount or type, that you will obtain. Also, your research questions won't be set in stone and will depend to a considerable extent on how things develop when doing your fieldwork. This makes it difficult to decide on the relevance of the various things that you have collected. Don't assume simply because you have collected some data that they have to be analysed. Researchers are only human. They find it difficult to jettison some aspect that they were keen on, particularly if they had to overcome problems in getting hold of the data, even when there appears to be little relevance to the questions they seek to answer. Ideally, once you realise that you are going down a blind alley in relation to how you now view your research questions, you will have cut your losses and have moved on to pursue things of greater relevance. However, it's almost inevitable that you end up with some unusable data. It might be possible to 'tweak' your research questions so the data become usable – but beware of the 'drunkard and lamp-post situation' (looking for a dropped watch under the lamp even though it was dropped somewhere else). Put it down to experience.

Quantitative (Numerical) Data

Data often either come as numbers or can be converted into numbers. Virtually all fixed designs, particularly experiments and surveys, yield such numerical data, but there are almost always some data of this type in a research project.

The techniques for summarizing and displaying data covered here can be useful for the simple quantitative data often collected as a minor aspect of flexible design research.

A good thing about quantitative data is that there are commonly agreed rules about how they should be dealt with. A bad thing, for the novice, is that there is a large, often complex, technology in the statistical analysis of these data. For the small-scale project on which this book focuses, there is rarely a need for complex statistical analysis. A possible exception is where you are focusing on a topic suggested by your supervisor that builds on previous work using complex analyses. These analyses then provide a model that you can follow.

The priority is to summarize and display your numerical data. Even in a small project, it is easy to end up with strings of numbers where it is very difficult to see the wood for the trees.

Some common situations producing different types of quantitative data are illustrated below by focusing on the demographic or 'background information' questions used to find out about the personal characteristics of respondents in questionnaires and other studies.

Categorical variables

One type of quantitative data is the numbers of responses, or whatever, that fall within different categories.

Situation 1: Responses fall into one or other of two categories. Example: the 'sex' question. Respondents are asked to tick a box indicating whether they are male or female. The variable we are interested in here is sex (an issue lurks here – some would use 'gender' rather than 'sex'; the former being viewed as a psychological/social construct, the latter as biological).

The kinds of analysis you can do include calculating the numbers falling in each category, and the relative proportions in the two categories (e.g. 60 per cent male, 40 per cent female). Appropriate types of statistical tests for this kind of data are discussed below on p. 128. In analysing the results of surveys, this type of data is sometimes coded (e.g. females are coded '1' and males '0'). The code numbers assigned are conventional and arbitrary (they could be females coded '0' and males '1' – or indeed any numbers you like).

Situation 2: Responses fall into one of several different categories. Example: current marital status. The question might be:

What is your current marital status? Please tick one of the boxes:

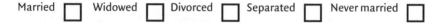

Married ☐ Widowed ☐ Divorced ☐ Separated ☐ Never married ☐

(There are complexities here which have to be thought about and instructions provided. For example, does 'marriage' include common-law or same sex marriages? Where does an annulment fit in?)

The same limited range of analyses is possible. Any coding is again arbitrary.

Ordered categorical variables

Situation 3: Responses fall into one of several different ordered categories. Example: *degree level performance.* In the UK it has been traditional to award first degrees in different 'classes', and the question might be:

What class of degree did you obtain? Please tick one of the boxes:

First ☐ Upper second ☐ Lower second ☐ Third ☐ Unclassified (pass degree) ☐

This is a further situation where a response falls into one of several different categories. However, the variable 'class of degree' can be ordered (i.e. a first class degree is at a higher level than an upper second, which is in turn higher than a lower second, etc.).

The same kinds of analysis are possible as in the two previous situations. There are also statistical tests known as non-parametric tests which can be used with categorical data.

Second example: *satisfaction ratings.* The same kind of data result from a commonly used 'satisfaction' question, e.g.

How do you rate your experience of the course so far? Please circle one:

Excellent   Very good   Good   Satisfactory   Poor   Very poor

This can, of course, be asked in many ways with different labels for the categories. Common to each of them is the idea that the responses can be ordered to indicate level of satisfaction. However, while the answers are often coded numerically (say, excellent = 7, very good = 6, good = 5: satisfactory = 4, poor = 3, very poor = 2, awful = 1) any such numbers are pretty much arbitrary and should be treated with caution. One difficulty is that we don't know the relative differences between the categories, only their order. Using numbers for the categories can mislead you into thinking that, say, a '6' represents twice the satisfaction of a '3'. More generally, any kind of arithmetical operation, such as working out or comparing average ratings of satisfaction (see below) is suspect and should be avoided. People who should know better often do this, however (you will see average ratings of this kind quoted in published journal articles).

Summarizing and displaying categorical data

The data can be displayed in the form of a table or bar chart as illustrated in Table 6.1 and Figure 6.1. The same data are presented in the table and the figure. For small amounts of data, there is not much to choose between the two. Figures, particularly with more complex or extensive data, probably communicate better to more audiences. The bar chart shown in Figure 6.1 is often used to display this kind of data but there are many alternatives which software such as Excel can easily generate.

Table 6.1 Class of degree obtained by respondents

Class of degree	First	Upper second	Lower second	Third	Unclassified
Frequency (number with class of degree)	4	18	12	3	3

Figure 6.1 Class of degree obtained by respondents

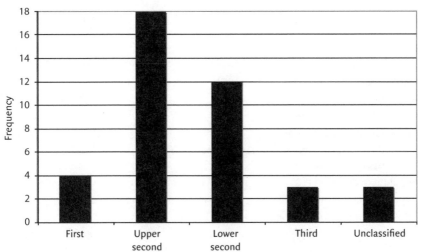

More complex displays can be produced by combining the responses from two or more questions or other sources of data. Table 6.2 combines data from a sex question and a 'main reason for choice of university' question. This is known as a cross-tabulation (sometimes as cross-classification). The table presents a cross-tabulation of the two-category sex response (male/female) and responses made when students at a sixth form college were asked to give their main reason for choice of university from a list of alternatives. The first

Table 6.2 Comparison of male and female main reasons for choice of university

Frequency (number giving that reason)		
Main reason for choice	*Females*	*Males*
Low cost of living	3	4
Nearness to home	25	7
Not near to home	0	13
Recommendation by friend	67	12
Recommendation by parent	12	5
Recommendation by school	15	22
Recommendation in a 'good university' guide or newspaper feature	19	39
Reputation for research	0	0
Reputation for teaching	4	0
University brochure or other advertising	93	103
Total	**238**	**205**

Within sex percentages		
Main reason for choice	*Females (%)*	*Males (%)*
Low cost of living	1.3	2.0
Nearness to home	10.5	3.4
Not near to home	0.0	6.3
Recommendation by friend	28.2	5.9
Recommendation by parent	5.0	2.4
Recommendation by school	6.3	10.7
Recommendation in a 'good university' guide or newspaper feature	8.0	19.0
Reputation for research	0.0	0.0
Reputation for teaching	1.7	0.0
University brochure or other advertising	39.1	50.2
Total	**100.0**	**100.0**

part of the table shows the numbers of males and females giving each of the alternatives as their main reason (these are called frequency counts). Statistical packages will produce such tables and also provide row and column totals and percentages. Percentages often show more clearly the pattern of results but you need to think carefully about what you want to know (and show). Here it probably makes more sense to display the distribution of reasons within sexes, i.e. the column percentages, as in the lower part of the table (for example 25 of the 238 females, or 10.5 per cent give 'nearness to home' as their main reason). This same information is displayed in Figure 6.2. Note that the ordering of the reasons for choice of university has been arranged to start with

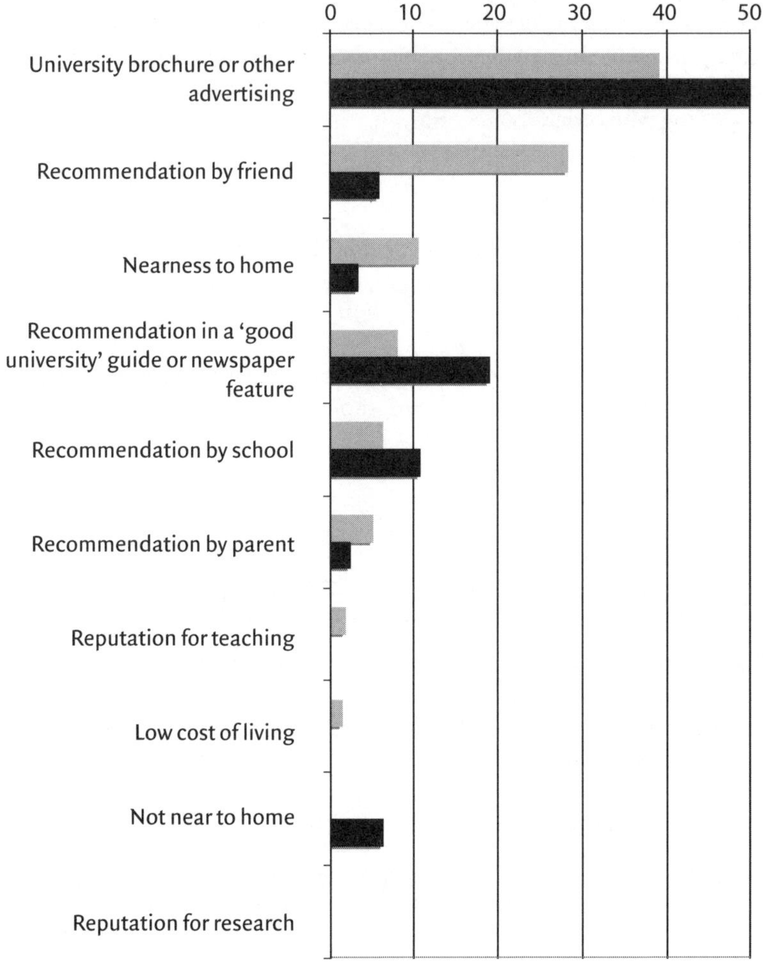

Figure 6.2 Comparison of male and female main reasons for choice of university

the most popular reasons and end with the least popular (ordering done on the basis of the female percentages – male percentages could have been used to sort out the order). This, perhaps, makes it somewhat easier to take in the information about the relative popularity of different reasons and of male/female differences. This change of order can be done because the original ordering of reasons as in Table 6.1 was arbitrary.

SPSS (the Statistical Package for the Social Sciences), and other packages, can also give the results of various statistical tests. The most commonly used in the situation shown in Table 6.2 is called Chi-square (χ^2). This provides a measure of the overall difference between the male and female distributions of reasons (in general terms the difference in row frequencies for the two columns). The larger the value of Chi-square, the bigger the difference in male and female opinions. This is a useful way of summarizing in a single figure much information about the data. Statistical packages can also provide a value for the statistical significance of the Chi-square value obtained (see below p. 125). Chi-square can be legitimately calculated for all categorical data, whether or not we are dealing with ordered categories.

Continuous variables

When you are measuring something that can, in principle, take on any value (examples are height, weight and age), this is known as a continuous or measured variable.

Situation: Responses can take on any value. Example: *the age question.* The question can be asked in different ways. For example, directly:

How old are you? ☐ years

or

What is your date of birth? | D D / M M / Y Y |

With this type of data you can carry out a range of analyses which are not feasible with categorical data.

When the age question is thought to be likely to be sensitive it might be put in terms of age groups:

What age group are you? Please tick one of the boxes:

Under 20 ☐   20–29 ☐   30–39 ☐   40–49 ☐   50–59 ☐   60 or above ☐

Asking the question in this way produces data in ordered categories ('20-year-olds', 30-year-olds', etc.). Continuous data can always be turned into ordered categorical data and this can be a useful way of summarizing and displaying large amounts of such data.

Calculating summary statistics with continuous variables

The most common type of summary statistic, and one of the most useful, is the simple average, known technically as the arithmetic mean. The idea of an average is well understood and communicates well. There are other ways of getting at what statisticians call the 'central tendency' of a set of figures which can be useful in particular circumstances (see below).

A second main way in which sets of numbers differ from each other is in the amount of variability or spread that they show. Two sets of figures can have the same average, but one might be tightly clustered about a central figure, while the other might be much more dispersed. There are various statistics that capture this aspect, including the range, standard deviation, and variance.

Once you have captured these two features of sets of numbers, you have a very useful short summary of their main characteristics.

Suppose we ask the 'age' question directly or by asking for dates of birth. Responses from 20 participants might be: 17, 20, 20, 20, 21, 23, 23, 23, 23, 24, 24, 24, 24, 25, 25, 26, 28, 30, 31, 45.

As with any data, the way you deal with them depends on what you want to know. Let us say that you are interested in the average age, perhaps to compare this group with some other group or groups. The arithmetic mean – sometimes simply referred to as the mean – is simply obtained by adding all the ages together and dividing by the number of responses:

Mean of the 20 responses = 24.8 years

Asking the age question in the form 'What age range are you in?' stops you from calculating the mean age in this way. You can work out an approximate figure by taking the mid-point of each age group and multiplying by the number of persons falling within that age group; then adding together the results from the different age groups. When a box like the 'under 20' or '60 and above' is used (which is useful as it ensures that all participants are included), a mid-point has to be guessed – say 15 and 65 respectively.

Here, the estimated mean, if the 20 responses had been entered into the different age range boxes, would be $(15 \times 1) + (24 \times 15) + (34 \times 2) + (45 \times 1)$ divided by 20. This is $488/20 = 24.4$. Which is an underestimate of the exact average of 24.8 years. A closer estimate would be obtained if you have prior knowledge of the likely age range of the respondents so you could fine tune the age ranges selected (here, for example, by using boxes of 'under 20', '20–24', '25–29', '30–34', and '35+'). This is one of the many aspects for which pilot work is invaluable.

Note that one of the 20 participants is considerably older than the rest, called by statisticians an *outlier*. Outliers, particularly if they are extreme, can lead to the arithmetic mean being not at all typical of the data.

Where there are extreme outliers, either very low or very high, or the set of scores appears markedly non-normal,* the *median* can provide a more sensible typical figure. The median is the middle value when a set of numbers is arranged in size order or the average of the two middle ones when you have an even number, as here. The median for this set of numbers is 24.[†]

Calculating variability

The variability or spread of a set of numerical responses to a question or whatever can be calculated in several ways. For data where the arithmetic mean is appropriate, the corresponding variability statistic is the standard deviation (or variance, which is the standard deviation squared). For anything other than very small amounts of data, this is tedious to calculate (see Robson, 1994 – available on the website – for details) and the use of a computer package such as Excel or SPSS is recommended.

When the median is appropriate as a measure of central tendency, it is usual to base the measure of variability on quartiles. Just as the median is the value in the middle of a set of numbers so that half of them are above and half below, the first quartile (Q_1) has a quarter of the numbers below (and three-quarters above) and the third quartile (Q_3) has three-quarters below and one-quarter above. The measure of variability is the inter-quartile range ($Q_3 - Q_1$) – or more commonly this is halved to give the semi-inter-quartile range ($Q_3 - Q_1$)/2. This isn't too difficult to work out by hand, or is straightforward using Excel or SPSS.

A somewhat different approach is to calculate the degree of confidence that a measure such as a mean or median falls within a particular range of values. This confidence interval is usually expressed as a percentage (often 95 per cent) and is again routinely calculated by statistical packages.

---

* Sets of scores are often close to a so-called 'normal' distribution. This is one where equal numbers of scores are above and below the arithmetic mean, and most of the scores are close to the mean with numbers tapering off as you get further from the mean.

† The 'mode' is also sometimes used. This is the most commonly occurring value – 23 years, occurring four times, is the mode for the age responses. The mode is useful as it can be legitimately used with categorical data. It is whatever category has the highest frequency (i.e. the category with the highest number of responses).

Table 6.3 Age distribution of participants

Age group	Number of participants
15–19 yrs	1
20–24 yrs	12
25–29 yrs	4
30–34 yrs	2
35+ yrs	1

Figure 6.3 Age distribution of participants

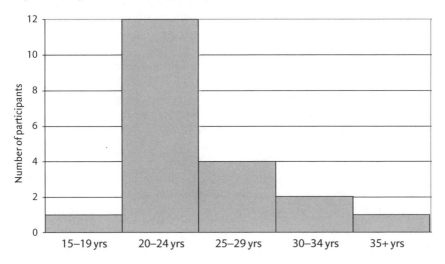

Displaying continuous variables

There are various ways of displaying the 'age' data. These include a simple table as illustrated in Table 6.3 and Figure 6.3. Note that Table 6.3 is set out differently from Table 6.1 – Table 6.1 has the different categories along the top; Table 6.3 presents them down the side. Either can be used. The type of bar chart in Figure 6.3, where the bars are touching, is sometimes known as a histogram and is conventionally used when, as here, the variable shown (age) is continuous.

Statistical tests and statistical significance

The answers to many research questions depend on being able to say something about mean scores, often about how means differ in different situations or conditions. Statistical tests (more exactly tests of statistical inference) can be used to assess the likelihood that your results could have been obtained if only chance factors were operating. For example, statistics known as t-tests can be used to assess the probability that a particular mean value differs from zero, or some other predicted or expected value, or of the difference obtained between mean values obtained under two conditions when only chance factors operate. This is known as assessing the statistical significance of your results. In some areas and disciplines (for example experimental psychology and medical science), this kind of assessment is considered essential. However:

☐ Statistical significance is a rather confusing and hence unfortunate, term. Simply because a result is statistically significant (i.e. unlikely to have happened by chance), neither says that it is significant – in the sense of being important – nor does it tell you directly why the result happened. There can be a whole host of non-chance factors that contribute to the results, depending on the design of your project.

☐ The chance of achieving a statistically significant result increases with the size of your study (i.e. the amount of data you collect). Statistical significance can be virtually guaranteed by carrying out a large enough study. So, paradoxically, a statistically significant result is more likely to be significant (important) if it is obtained in a small study!

☐ The statistical tests used to assess statistical significance make assumptions about the nature of the data collected. In practice, many of these assumptions are often violated, casting doubt on the meaning of the test results. Non-parametric tests have fewer assumptions about the nature of the data but the problem of interpreting statistical significance remains.

Effect sizes

An approach that avoids many of the problems associated with statistical significance is to calculate effect sizes. For example, in the situation where a comparison is made between mean scores obtained under two conditions, an effect size can be found by dividing the difference in means by a measure of the variability in the data (the statistic known as Cohen's d can be used). Comparisons can then be made between the sizes of effect found in different studies.

Confidence intervals (see above, p. 124) can also be used. Suppose that the 95 per cent confidence interval for a mean under one condition is, say, between 14.2 and 16.5, and for a second condition is between 17.1 and 20.6. Because there is no overlap it is unlikely that the difference in means is due to chance factors.

In situations where there is an expectation that you measure statistical significance, it is good practice to also provide effect sizes. This is easy to do when using statistical packages.

Clinical significance

However, even effect sizes do not really tell you much about how significant (in the sense of being meaningful or important) a finding is. This is called clinical significance from its use in medical and related settings. At root, it is not an issue that can be determined by statistical analysis. It is a judgement that has to be made by those with an interest in the findings and their use, whether they are consumers, professionals, managers, other researchers, examiners, or whoever. Your job, as discussed in the following chapter on writing up the research, is to make it clear what your findings are and to present your interpretation of their meaning and implications. You have exactly the same task whether you are dealing with quantitative or qualitative data (as discussed later in the chapter).

What test do I use?

As well as tests for means, there is a huge range of statistical tests for just about any situation where you are analysing numerical data. And there are computer packages such as SPSS which can make the task of analysis deceptively easy. Beware! Unless you know what you are doing, it is all too easy to generate impressive looking garbage. Table 6.4 lists some of the more common tests and what they are used for. Research questions often boil down to asking whether there are differences between things or whether there are relationships between them. For example, in a study of driving behaviour we might be interested in finding out whether there are differences between male and female performance (say, do male drivers take more risks than female drivers?). Another study might focus on whether there is a relationship between number of years of driving experience and the risks taken. Figure 6.4 illustrates how the results of a study might appear. The display shown is known as a scatter plot. It can be seen that there is a tendency for more risks to be taken by those with less experience, and fewer risks by those with more experience. Relationships of this type between measures or variables are known as correlations. Correlation coefficients provide a simple and useful way of describing the strength of such relationships. For the data shown, the appropriate correlation coefficient (the 'Pearson product-moment correlation') is computed as −0.65. The minus sign indicates that we have an inverse relationship. High values on one measure (risk) tend to be paired with low values on the other (experience) and vice-versa. Correlation coefficients range from +1 to −1, with the mid-point 0 indicating no relationship. Statistical significance levels can be computed and tell you how likely it is to get the observed coefficient if there is zero correlation between the variables.

Table 6.4 Choosing an appropriate statistical test

A Research questions about relationships

Categorical data	**Continuous data**
Two variables	*Two variables*
a) categories not ordered: contingency coefficient	Pearson product-moment correlation
b) ordered categories: Kendall rank correlation	
More than two variables	*More than two variables*
a) categories not ordered: discriminant analysis	Multiple regression analysis
b) ordered categories: Kendall partial rank correlation	

B Research questions about differences

Categorical data	**Continuous data**
Two variables	*Two variables*
a) categories not ordered	i) related samples t-test (correlated samples)
i) related samples: McNemar test	ii) independent samples t-test (independent samples)
ii) independent samples: Chi-square	
b) ordered categories	
i) related samples: Wilcoxon test	
ii) independent samples: Mann-Whitney test	
More than two variables	*More than two variables*
a) categories not ordered	Analysis of variance (type of analysis depends on design)
i) related samples: Cochran Q test	
ii) independent samples: Chi-square	
b) ordered categories	
i) related samples: Friedman two-way analysis of variance	
ii) independent samples: Kruskal-Wallis one-way analysis of variance	

Table 6.4 also lists statistical tests that can be used in more complex designs where you have more than two variables (e.g. in the example above you might have results for several different measures of risk-taking, or you might have measures not only of risk but also, say, of driving skill as well).

Figure 6.4 Scatter plot showing relationship between driving experience and risks taken

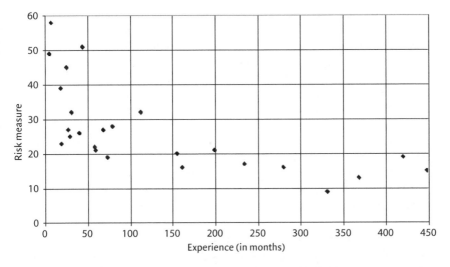

Unless you already have skills and experience in using statistical tests, you are strongly advised to seek advice from someone who has. Not every researcher can be expected to be an expert in the analysis of data, and an important skill to be developed as a budding researcher is how and when to use the skills of others.

The question to ask yourself is 'do I really need to use statistical tests?' The answer is probably 'yes' if there is a strong expectation in your field of work (and by your supervisor) of using such tests. However, even in such situations, you need to satisfy yourself, firstly, that the tests actually add anything to your interpretation of the results and, secondly, whether or not the tests can legitimately be used in the circumstances of your study. You are the one to decide the former issue, but you will probably need advice from someone with statistical expertise for the latter one. It is worse to use a statistic wrongly than not use one at all. There is much misuse of statistical tests – even in published journal articles.

In many small-scale research projects, simple summary or descriptive statistics, such as the mean and variance, convey much of the information you need. When supported by tables, bar charts and other displays of your data, they go a long way toward providing what you need to form the basis of your interpretation and to assist your reader to understand your findings and their value.

Qualitative Data

Many projects involve the collection of some qualitative, non-numerical data, most probably in the form of words. Responses to questions in interviews, notes that you make when observing and documents typically produce verbal outcomes. Qualitative data may be a small contribution within an essentially quantitatively-oriented study, or they may form central features of your study.

They aren't necessarily verbal and can, for example, be in the form of still or moving images: photographs, pictures, drawings, video, etc. Their analysis calls for specialized treatment (see references on the website).

Some qualitative data can be transformed into numbers. It can be possible and useful to develop a set of categories, work out which category a verbal response falls into and then count the frequency (i.e. the number of times) different categories are used. Such transformed data can then be summarized and displayed using the methods discussed in the previous section on quantitative data analysis.

However, much verbal data has a richness and complexity that cannot be captured by such processes. The challenge is to find ways of dealing with qualitative data that do them justice. This is a topic of much interest currently, evidenced by there being a plethora of texts written covering the analysis of qualitative data in the last two decades. One problem is that there is no single agreed way of going about this. Alternatives abound, typically linked to particular views about the kind of theoretical stance to adopt. It is not feasible to do justice to even a small number of these approaches in this kind of text (the further reading section provides references).

Most approaches, however, depend on your finding ways of reducing and organizing the data.

Data reduction and organization

Qualitative data, whether interview transcripts, notes from observational sessions, or whatever, tend to be voluminous. To get a grip on what you have, you almost always need to reduce its volume, to organize and condense it into something more manageable. In carrying out this whole data reduction and organization process, take care not to distance yourself from the original data. The interpretation and understanding of qualitative data can be crucially dependent on their context.

In one sense, you have already done a major job of 'anticipatory' data reduction at the design stage of your study, by the choices you make about 'who', 'when' and 'where'. You only obtain data from a limited number of people, at specified times and in particular places, determined by your research questions and the resources at your disposal.

Editing Once you have some data, its reduction to something you can deal with is an important part of the data analysis. You edit out 'dross' – sections of interviews where respondents go off on an irrelevant topic – discarding irrelevant documents. Don't throw such stuff away though. You may find that your focus changes so that something initially not wanted becomes relevant.

Summarizing Producing summaries is invaluable. It not only reduces the amount of data, but producing the summary forces you to attend to the data closely. Keep the full data, of course; you may need verbatim quotations for your account.

Coding This involves splitting the data into units or segments that seem to you to be relevant and meaningful. It helps to bear your research questions in mind when starting on this task so that you can pick up anything relevant in the data. However, try to remain open to other aspects that seem to be present and of interest. Remember that the research questions are not set in stone and that the data may be giving answers to rather different questions to those you had originally.

You are looking for small chunks of material that might be put into categories, which can be provisionally labelled or named, and for wider themes and patterns which help organize the categories. As suggested above, this system may be derived from the data themselves, perhaps combined with categories and themes suggested by your previous reading and the research questions. The basic strategy is to compare and contrast in order to find those things that seem to be similar and those that seem to be different. Be prepared to modify and change the categories and the way you organize them. You must retain flexibility as you get in more data and/or develop different insights about what you have.

It is common for those doing this analysis for the first time to over-code and end up with an unmanageable number of codes and sub-codes. As your understanding of the data grows, you may feel the need to review, and probably simplify, your set of codes. Don't be afraid of using direct quotations from participants as codes where this seems appropriate (and certainly ensure that you keep tabs on useful quotations so that they help illuminate and make vivid your account in the project report).

Memoing This means writing memos to yourself reflecting insights, thoughts and hunches about the data. This not only helps to understand what you have got but also to ensure that you don't forget things. Memos also provide a useful record to show the process you have followed in dealing with the data.

Conceptualizing At a later stage, the move is to conceptualize what you have found. How can the themes and patterns, which may change as more data are analysed, best be understood?

Displaying As with quantitative data, displays of various kinds are a powerful way of reducing and organizing qualitative data. These include matrices, the equivalent of cross-tabulation, where two lists are set up as the rows and columns of a table. Figure 6.5 gives an example. The columns represent a sequence of stages in a project focusing on facilitating the entry of socially and economically disadvantaged students into university education. The rows cover different levels in the school system where the project intervened. The matrix provides a means of condensing much information from field notes into a single display. Supposing that matrices were produced for each of three case study schools, then this facilitates comparisons of the similarities and differences between the contexts.

Other possible displays include flow-charts and networks illustrating relationships and structures, typically by showing boxes and connections between them. The following section goes into more detail about one widely used approach to the analysis of qualitative data.

Figure 6.5 Matrix of issues and concerns by phase and level

Level	Phase				
	A	B	C	D	E
Local authority					
Head and senior management					
Class teachers					
Mentors					
Students					
Parents					

An example – the grounded theory approach to analysis

Grounded theory is both an overall theoretical approach to doing research (seeking theory which is 'grounded' in, or derived from, the data you have collected), as discussed in chapter 2, p. 39, and a set of procedures for data analysis and interpretation.

It is essentially a three-step procedure. *Open coding* comes first – it is open in the sense of 'opening up' the data, splitting it up into small chunks and labelling (coding) them . You give the same label to those chunks that seem to be conceptually similar. A distinctive feature of the grounded theory approach is that right from the start you are looking for abstract theoretical categories that help you to make sense of the data. The 'what is going on here?' question is up front. The codes or labels are provisional. You may need to change them as you get and analyse more data.

There is much to be said for doing this with a colleague, perhaps someone who also has qualitative data to analyse, so that you can help them out later. It helps to keep you honest, through having to defend your coding to a critical friend, and you can spark ideas off each other. If this isn't feasible, you should go through your analyses in detail afterwards with someone.

At this open coding stage you should alternate between detailed, intensive scrutiny of sections of the data and standing back to try to keep in mind the bigger picture. This will not only help to confirm or modify your thoughts about what the appropriate categories are, but also start to give ideas about how the individual categories might be grouped together and classified, and (the overall goal of grounded theory) what might be the core high-level category central in the data.

The second step is referred to as *theoretical coding*. Here, the task is to find ways of inter-relating the various categories produced through open coding. There are major disagreements between different proponents of grounded theory about how this should be done. The purist wing insist that these codes must emerge solely from studying the data, others take a more relaxed view. My own preference is to acknowledge that it is difficult, if not impossible (and probably undesirable anyway), to approach this task with a totally open mind. Your 'previous', i.e. what you bring to the analysis through prior reading and experience, and in particular your research questions, necessarily predisposes you to look for particular kinds of relationships.

The final step is *selective coding*. This involves deciding on a core category. What is the central focus around which we can best integrate the data? Details and examples of grounded theory are provided in the book by Strauss and Corbin listed in the further reading section at the end of the chapter. The website gives links to research that uses the approach.

Grounded theory, though widely used, is just one of a plethora of approaches to the analysis of qualitative data – see the further reading section.

Using specialist computer packages for qualitative data analysis

There are several specialist packages which can help you make use of a computer to carry out an analysis of qualitative data (see the website for details). At the time of writing a widely used system is known as NUD•IST – the somewhat provocative acronym stands for non-numerical, unstructured data indexing, searching and theorizing. A variant known as NVivo is becoming increasingly popular. Whereas using statistical software such as SPSS with quantitative data is strongly recommended for all but the most simple statistical analysis, whether or not to go for computer-assisted qualitative data analysis is a more difficult decision.

It is only worthwhile if you have a substantial amount of qualitative data to analyse, and you are prepared to devote a considerable amount of time to gain facility in using the software. It is particularly worthwhile if you are going on to other projects producing qualitative data, and/or consider it a useful addition to your CV.

NUD•IST, NVivo and other packages are essentially aids to carrying out the tasks you would be carrying out for yourself if you were doing the analysis by hand (working with interview transcripts, documents or whatever, coding and labelling different segments, sorting them out in various ways using highlighters, cutting and pasting, etc.). You don't, as it were, push a button and find the answer magically printed out as you do with SPSS. The software helps you to carry out the various tasks more systematically and provides various aids to displaying and summarizing your findings.

However, there is still a lot to be said for doing qualitative data analysis as a purely paper exercise. If you feel happier fixing big sheets of paper to the wall with felt-tip flow-charts and other diagrams, post-it notes of various colours, etc., then go for it. It doesn't have to be an all-or-none decision. One possibility is to do your coding, and some key figures, using NVivo, then move on to the 'sheets of paper on the wall' mode.

Summary of qualitative data analysis

Following the above principles should help you produce a worthwhile analysis. The procedure cannot be routinized in the kind of way that a statistical analysis of quantitative data can be. Because of this, it is a challenging task that can be daunting. It is very helpful to have advice and support from someone who has experience with this type of analysis. The website provides examples of a range of qualitative data analyses of a variety of styles.

The good news (and the bad news) is that there is no single 'right way' of doing qualitative data analysis. Take with a pinch of salt the advice of those who say that 'you must use X' – where X is ethnomethodology, or discourse analysis, or deconstruction, or even the grounded theory approach focused on here. By all means, buy into a particular theoretical perspective and analytic system if you understand it and if it fits in with the purposes of your project.

Providing that you have approached the analysis in a systematic and disciplined manner and that you have provided sufficient detail so that a reader can get an answer to the question 'how did she get from these data to these conclusions?', you are in the clear.

Interpretation – What Is Going on Here?

This text emphasizes the importance of coming up with one or more specific research questions and of designing your project so that you are in a position to get answers to these questions. However, underlying the vast majority of projects lurks a more general or fundamental question – What is going on here? How do I interpret, understand or explain the findings of my project?

This is most obviously the central over-arching question when the project has an explicit explanatory purpose. It is still on the agenda when the project is descriptive or exploratory. Suppose your main research question concerns the relative numbers of boys and girls with particular types of special needs (such as, for example, learning or behaviour difficulties) in schools and you find that there are more boys than girls with such needs in the schools you survey. Incidentally, international statistics commonly find an approximate 60 per cent male to 40 per cent female split (OECD, 2004; pp. 109–13). Or you might have carried out an exploratory study where such a finding arises from your involvement in schools. While this information is valuable in its own right, raising issues about equity and the distribution of scarce resources, the 'what is going on here' question is inescapable.

Several possibilities might be suggested. Perhaps boys are more vulnerable than girls. It is known that certain disabilities are sex-linked, with boys more likely to be affected than girls. A very different explanation comes from suggestions that schooling is being increasingly 'feminized' (with, particularly at primary level, an increasing scarcity of male teachers) such that boys find it more difficult to fit in with the prevailing ethos. This might then lead to boys exhibiting more behavioural problems in the classroom – and being labelled as having 'special needs'. Another school-related factor might be linked to increased emphases being placed on the need for academic learning in schools in countries such as the United Kingdom where the position of schools in academic league tables is highly visible. Girls might outperform boys in areas such as literacy, resulting in boys again being judged as having special needs because of learning difficulties. A different social or cultural explanation might be that a society places more emphasis on the education of boys and hence their needs are given priority.

The philosophical stance known as realism* provides a useful language for talking about these issues. The possibilities or factors discussed above are referred to as 'mechanisms'. Unfortunately, mechanism is viewed as something of a dirty word in some social research and other quarters. When the word is seen as meaning the 'construction of a machine', this view is understandable.

---

* There are several versions of realism including scientific realism, critical realism and subtle realism (Danermark et al., 2002).

However, the dictionary definition as 'an arrangement or action by which a result is obtained' is less provocative. Similarly 'mechanistic explanations' carry negative connotations whereas the meaning is simply 'explanations in terms of mechanisms'. The term is not really important. Substitute 'factor' or another synonym if 'mechanism' grates on you. However, the quest for an answer to the 'why' question is important. Realism not only provides this emphasis but also stresses that their mechanisms are 'underlying', that you are not limited to talking about things that can be directly observed and that one shouldn't expect mechanisms to operate for all situations or contexts, or for all people involved in a particular intervention. When studying some social situation, innovation, intervention or whatever, it is often not helpful or appropriate to be looking for general overall effects. What you are after is 'what works, for whom, and in what context' (Pawson and Tilley, 1997).

Because applied social research, in fields such as evaluation, has been plagued by weak, commonly inconsistent, overall findings, this changed perspective provides a welcome lifeline.

Realism stresses that mechanisms can operate at different levels, including the biological, psychological, social and societal levels. Thus, in the educational example given above, biological mechanisms may well be effective in relation to specific disabilities. Psychological, individual person level, mechanisms may operate resulting in emotional or behavioural difficulties being expressed. The school and classroom climate may reflect the operation of social or group mechanisms, while societal mechanisms may result in differential priorities being given to male and female education.

To which you might legitimately complain that this is so complicated that I am never going to be able to sort out what mechanisms or factors are operating in a particular study. Well, I never promised it would be easy. Anything involving people (i.e. all social research whether pure or applied) is inherently complicated.

Don't despair. The task becomes more manageable when you appreciate that you are not being asked to come up with definitive, copper-bottomed answers from a small-scale project. Science, particularly social science, isn't like that. Even the best designed and executed project can only, at best, just put 'another brick in the wall'. That is, it has to be seen in the context of other research and, generally, what is known and understood about a particular field or topic.

The good news is that, with sufficient thought, ingenuity and persistence, it ought to be possible to say something sensible about 'what is going on here' after any even half-way reasonable project. What is at issue is how plausible and believable a tale you can tell. Some designs make this task easier. If you already have a good idea about what is going on, from previous research and from the views and experience of people who have been closely involved, or whatever, then you can carry out a closely focused study putting your ideas to the test. An experimental design might be called for in this situation.

However, we often don't have the degree of pre-knowledge about these matters that would make an experiment a good bet. Or the situation might not lend itself to the degree of control needed in experimentation. Or your specific research questions, or the kind of project you feel comfortable with carrying out, could rule experiments out.

Further Reading

Charmaz, K. C. (2005) *Grounded Theory for the 21st Century*. London and Thousand Oaks, CA: Sage. Practical introduction with good range of worked examples. Doesn't follow the Glaser and Strauss line closely.

Clark-Carter, D. (2004) *Quantitative Psychological Research Textbook: A student's handbook.* 2nd edition. London: Psychology Press. Hefty handbook with wide coverage of aspects of analysing quantitative data. Very clearly presented.

Coffey, A. and Atkinson, P. (1996) *Making Sense of Qualitative Data: Complementary research strategies*. London and Thousand Oaks, CA: Sage. Covers a range of approaches to analysing qualitative data. Invaluable if you aren't sure which to take.

Gibbs, G. R. (2002) *Qualitative Data Analysis: Explorations with NVivo*. Buckingham: Open University Press. Covers the use of NVivo with several approaches to qualitative analysis including grounded theory. Clearly and logically presented.

Hinton, P. R., Brownlow, C., McMurray, I. and Cozens, B. (2004) *SPSS Explained*. London: Taylor and Francis. Useful for both basic and advanced analyses. Clear guidance through all steps in the process for input to output. Includes wide range of statistical tests and the use of SPSS to analyse questionnaires.

Mason, J. (2002) *Qualitative Researching*. 2nd edition. London and Thousand Oaks, CA: Sage. Very clear and accessible. Covers all aspects of qualitative researching as well as analysis.

Punch, K. F. (2005) *Introduction to Social Research: Quantitative and qualitative approaches*. 2nd edition. London and Thousand Oaks, CA: Sage. Detailed and very clear coverage of both quantitative and qualitative approaches to analysis of data.

Robson, C. (1994) *Experiment, Design and Statistics in Psychology*. 3rd edition. Harmondsworth: Penguin. Covers simple statistical tests and ways of summarizing quantitative data. Full text available free from author's Blackwell website (www.blackwellpublishing.com/robson/ebook.htm).

Strauss, A. and Corbin, J. (1998) *Basics of Qualitative Research: Techniques and procedures for developing grounded theory*. London and Thousand Oaks, CA:

Sage. A practical introduction to qualitative analysis using the grounded theory approach. *Note:* Computer packages for both quantitative and qualitative data analysis regularly appear in revised and updated versions. The principles of NVivo and SPSS packages are likely to remain the same but you may have to use online manuals to cover new features.

Chapter 6 Tasks

Note: Following a flexible design, much of your data is likely to be qualitative in the form of words, but there are usually some numbers to be dealt with. A fixed design typically generates quantitative data in the form of numbers but can benefit from the use of a secondary data collection method that may well generate some words.

Seek help and advice with the carrying out the following tasks:

1 *Decide how you will handle the quantitative data.* Decide on what are appropriate ways of dealing with the quantitative data you have collected. In all cases, you need to know how to summarize and display these data. You may need to carry out statistical tests, particularly in fixed-design research.

2 *If you propose using statistical tests, familiarize yourself with SPSS (or another statistical analysis package).* Make sure that you know not only how to enter data and run the analysis, but also that you understand what the output means. Check this by running the analysis with pilot, or fictitious, data.

3 *Decide how you will handle the qualitative data.* Small amounts of such data do not call for sophisticated treatment but, if you have a substantial amount, use some system (e.g. the grounded theory approach) for coding and interpreting the data. Make sure you understand what it involves.

4 *Decide whether or not you are going to use NVivo (or some other package) to analyse your qualitative data.* If you are, you need to familiarize yourself with the package.

5 *Go through these tasks before the main data collection exercise.* You don't want to be faced with a lot of data you don't know what to do with.

7

Writing the Report

The advice presented in chapter 1 was to make a start by writing drafts of parts of the report early in the research process. The most obvious bit to start on is the one giving the background to your choice of topic and discussion of relevant existing material and research – often called the 'literature review'. Once you have made decisions about the general approach to be taken, the research design and the data collection methods, a start can also be made on these aspects – sometimes referred to as the 'methodology' section. Similarly, you will need to have given serious thought to the possible ethical issues raised by your project before data collection starts, so this can be discussed.

Any writing of this kind that you can do is good psychologically. You can see that progress is being made. Almost inevitably, you will be tight up to deadlines for completion of the project at the end, so any material you can accumulate earlier helps. However, you have to be prepared to redraft (probably several times). Your findings and their interpretation will usually mean that the earlier stages have to be revisited in order to make sure that they 'fit'. Many people find it difficult to delete sections that are no longer relevant. However, just because you have written it doesn't mean it has to be in the final version of the report.

There can also be advantage in producing tentative drafts of the later parts of the report where you provide an interpretation of your findings before you have completed the data collection and analysis. This is, of course, not an invitation to invent fictitious results. Researchers often have a pretty good idea about what the findings will be (or perhaps have two or three likely scenarios of what they will find). Writing up an interpretation will help you judge the strength or weakness of your research argument. It will also help to make apparent any gaps that need to be plugged by collecting additional data or completing additional analyses.

Planning and Drafting

I am sure that, for nearly everybody, although this might be your first research report, it won't be your first report or written assignment. While there are some specific features of research reports, which are covered below, good reports of whatever kind share common features. They are:

☐ clearly structured
☐ lucidly written
☐ professionally presented (which includes standard spelling, punctuation and referencing), and
☐ your own work.

As with any transition in the research process, there is a tendency to procrastinate when faced with the report-writing task. I'll start next week. I really ought to read a few more books, journal articles, other reports, etc. Or I'm sure that I could get more out of my data if I kept working at them. Or I would do a better quality job if I had a short holiday. Or . . . All of which may have some truth but if you don't start, you don't finish. So give yourself a realistic deadline which will leave sufficient time to make a good job of the report. You will never be perfectly prepared to write, but you must give yourself the chance of making the best of what you have got.

Different people approach the task of writing the research report in different ways. However, everyone should have a plan of some kind before starting writing. The issue is whether to just have something very sketchy or something on which you spend a lot of time trying to get the structure down in considerable detail. If you feel more secure following the latter path, then fine. However, it can be another ruse to put off the writing itself. And if you do go for a detailed plan, it is important to be prepared to modify it as you go on. Box 7.1 shows a possible structure. However, it is very important that you follow the structure expected in your field or discipline. Don't give examiners an excuse for marking you down on something that is easy to get right. Course handbooks usually include guidelines on the structure and type of presentation expected, including length. Reports of previous projects should be available. Find a good one that you like and which has similarities to your project. Use it as a model. This is particularly useful if your project isn't mainstream (perhaps you have followed a flexible design which, while permissible, is not typical).

A plan helps a writer to jump the 'getting started' hurdle. At least you have a heading, not just a blank page or screen staring back at you. If you are stuck with one section, it's always possible to turn to another one. There is, of course, no rule that says you have to proceed in a linear fashion, following section 1 with section 2, etc. Why not start by writing a section where you have a pretty strong notion of how you are going to treat it? As discussed above, it is

Box 7.1 A possible report structure

1 Title page Title, including subtitle. Your name and date.

2 Acknowledgements You acknowledge the help you have received (don't forget to mention a helpful supervisor!).

3 Contents This lists the section headings and subheadings, giving their page numbers. You should also provide a list of any figures or tables, and of any appendices, again with page numbers.

4 Abstract See p. 148. Keep to any word limits.

5 Introduction This outlines what you have done in the project, why and how. It gives a brief background and states the ethical issues, the research questions and the limitations of the study.

6 Literature review This gives the context of, and background to, your study. It covers relevant previous research.

7 Methodology This details the general approach taken, the design of the project and the choice of methods. In fixed-design research, it is expected that sufficient detail is provided for a reader to carry out an exact replication of your study. The ethical issues anticipated and encountered are outlined.

8 Results This gives the presentation of the data, and the analysis and interpretation of your findings.

9 Discussion This gives the answers to research questions and general discussion about the project and your findings. Also included are relations to earlier findings, limitations, implications, improvements and suggestions for further research, recommendations for change (where appropriate) and the dissemination of results.

10 References This provides a full list of all works referred to in the report. See p. 147.

11 Appendices This includes copies of questionnaires and other research instruments (samples only) and any other relevant material (e.g. transcripts of interviews).

Note: Check if a particular structure is expected on your course. Use that structure. Regard the above as an aide-mémoire of things to include at some point in the report.

comforting to have something, at least provisionally, in the bag. When you get a full draft, you are going to have to revisit sections you wrote at an early stage to try to make sure that everything fits together – probably deleting some parts you were initially quite proud of because they don't fit in with the way things turned out.

Given some kind of plan, my own preference is to 'splurge' when writing; i.e. to get stuck into the task and try to keep the words coming at a good rate, not worrying at this stage about style, clarity, spelling and punctuation. Others are unhappy with this strategy, preferring to try to produce a pretty clean draft version as they are writing.

When starting to plan your research report, you should have your research questions in front of you, literally as well as metaphorically. They may still be the original ones you started out with when preparing for your project as covered in Part I of this text. Quite possibly they will have changed and developed along the way. You should also have some, at least tentative, answers to these questions from the analysis of your data.

Some people like the security of having the structure of their report sorted out at a quite early stage. There is nothing wrong with this and it can help with time planning. However, you should be prepared to revisit the structure, as well as the content, as you get a clearer idea of what you are getting out of the research data. Also, with a flexible design, you will be carrying out some data analysis and interpretation along the way to help decide how later data collection goes. An account of this process is a legitimate contribution to the report. It helps readers to understand the journey you have taken when doing the project, and strengthens the trustworthiness of your findings.

Whatever your design, there will be elements of your report which you can work on almost from day one of your involvement in the project. There are usually times when you find that you can't make progress on data collection, perhaps because you are waiting for an approval of some kind. Or where you get fed up with working on analysing data. As the old adage goes, 'a change is as good as a rest'.

Research Arguments

When writing a research report, you are essentially presenting an argument (in the sense of evidence or proof, rather than a dispute). Booth et al. (2003; chapter 7) in their text, *The Craft of Research*, devote a chapter to 'making good arguments'. They are writing from a background in the humanities but suggest that there is a common set of elements to all research arguments. Central to such arguments are claims, reasons and evidence.

Claims

Booth and his colleagues distinguish between the main claim and claims in general. The main claim is seen most clearly in a doctoral dissertation. The thesis, although sometimes regarded as another word meaning dissertation, is more strictly the main claim made. A common question at a doctoral oral examination is 'So what, exactly, is your thesis?' The candidate is expected to come up with a sentence or two explaining the main claim that their dissertation supports.

Similarly, in all other research reports, you should end up with one or more (probably not more than half a dozen, at the outside) main claims. If you have followed the research question route, these are your answers to these questions. One of the advantages of thinking in terms of research questions is that it keeps you focused on the claims you are going to be making.

Any research report should also be stuffed throughout with what might be called mini-claims. For example, in producing a literature review or review of previous research, you make a range of claims about what the previous work shows, how it can be understood and why and how it is relevant to your own research. When interpreting the data that you have analysed, you again come up with a range of claims for which you have to demonstrate support. In getting to the stage of providing answers to your research questions, there are likely to be several underlying claims to be evaluated.

Reasons and evidence

Booth and his colleagues distinguish between reasons and evidence in supporting claims. In the simplest form you

> [make a claim] because of [a reason]

For example I read in a newspaper the claim that there is increased incidence of anti-social behaviour and aggression in children aged three, because of the use of day nurseries for children under two. The distinctive feature of research is the requirement to provide the evidence, usually in the form of data, on which the reason is based. In other words, you

> [make a claim] because of [a reason] based on [evidence]

In the childcare example, there is clear evidence from research studies, in both America and the United Kingdom, of linked increases in later anti-social behaviour for those children who had attended day nurseries at an early age (Sylva et al., 2004). However, it is something of a leap to move from the link (more time in day nursery below two years associated with greater anti-social behaviour at three) to the 'because'.

If we are solely concerned with description, then the link or association might be as far as we want to go. The stress might be on getting firm evidence of the strength of the link or perhaps to get a more detailed description of differences associated with the time spent in the nursery and the quality of the provision (staff/children ratios, staff turnover and qualifications, etc.). Such purely descriptive research effectively says 'don't bother me with reasons, just give me the facts'. It can be represented as

[make a descriptive claim] based on [evidence]

In practice, even descriptive researchers are tempted into making causal statements. They can cover themselves to some extent by stressing the tentative nature of any 'because' statements they make. And, of course, any such statements arising from a single research project (particularly a small-scale one) are inevitably tentative to a greater or lesser extent.

How, then, does one persuade the reader about the likely truth of your 'because'? As discussed in the previous chapter, p. 135, the realist approach talks in terms of *mechanisms*. Just as the claims you make are the answers to your research questions, so the reasons are mechanisms. In crude terms, they are the things going on which provide an explanation for what you have found.

In the childcare example Dr Penelope Leach (co-director, with Professors Kathy Silva and Alan Stein, of the largest UK study of childcare from birth to school age, Families, Children and Child Care FCC, www.familieschildren-childcare.org) argues that an important mechanism is 'insecure attachment' by the infant to an adult. She marshals evidence from a range of studies in support of this. For example, staff in nurseries have been shown to be detached, less sensitive and responsive toward the children, with an undifferentiated response to different children. She cites the importance of very large amounts of individual attention in developing attachment, linking this to research showing that non-group based care as provided by childminders and nannies is not associated with later increased anti-social behaviour. The study quoted above looked directly at insecure attachment and found that having more than 10 hours of nursery day-care a week in the first year was a major risk factor.

Booth et al. (2003; chapter 7) not only talk in terms of claims, reasons and evidence, but also add the need to acknowledge and respond to alternatives. You are inevitably selective in the reasons you cite and the evidence you use. It is necessary to cover alternatives. This is relatively easier when these are reasons that you have discarded or evidence that you have discounted. You say why in order to justify your choices. The difficult part is to try to anticipate other alternatives that you had previously not thought about. This is best dealt with by having colleagues critique drafts of your report, where you have given them the task of suggesting alternative explanations.

The approach advocated here provides a useful framework for structuring your research argument and ensuring that it all hangs together. You can, with profit, supplement this structured discussion of the findings with a more free-flowing account of what you have learned from the project. A modicum of creative speculation doesn't come amiss.

Considering Your Audience(s) Again

Presenting the research argument can be thought of as a conversation with the reader of your report. The audience for a research report is usually considered to be those working in the field or discipline that your research focuses on. Not specialists in the particular topic of your study, but those with a general background and interest in education, nursing, social psychology, or wherever your focus lies. For an undergraduate research project, your direct audience is the people who are going to examine it. In practice, degree regulations often refer to the model of the research report or journal article, so that tells you what to aim at.

My audience in writing this book is you, the undergraduate student faced with the task of successfully completing the final year research project. To that end I have written in a relatively informal and, I hope, accessible style. This style would not be appropriate for many research project reports. A solemnity is often expected, particularly in quantitative projects. There are, however, growing signs of growing acceptance of a more lively and engaging written style.

The general message is that consideration of audience expectations should influence your report's style and content. A simple strategy is to find a model (or preferably a few different ones) in the form of existing reports you think do the job well. Select ones where there is evidence that it is highly regarded. Perhaps your supervisor recommends it, and/or it got a high grade, and/or it's published in a reputable journal or other outlet.

As discussed in chapter 1, p. 9, you may be trying to reach a different audience. For an in-house study, this might be the managing director or personnel manager. For a report on a local initiative, this might be the team running it. While this will strongly influence the approach you take and, importantly, the language and length of the report, your job is essentially the same. You are making clear what you are claiming or, put in other terms, what your findings are. Also you are providing reasons, with evidence, supporting your claim.

In a situation where audiences of this kind just want to focus on the findings, or even on recommendations arising from them, there is nothing wrong with giving them what they ask for. However don't let this be an excuse for your avoiding the hard slog of following through the full research argument to ensure that you are making a justifiable claim. A good strategy here when, say, the boss just wants an executive summary on one sheet, followed by a very short report, is to include all the rest in a set of appendices or annexes. This not only salves your research conscience, but also makes it clear that she is getting a lot of output for her money. By colour-coding the pages of appendices, they can be easily avoided by the time-poor.

You may end up needing to produce more than one report. This is often the case when doing applied research for an award or qualification. Here your prime audience is the examiner and you have to follow the rules and regulations for the award. However, if, as is often the case, you also wish to communicate to (and, hopefully, influence) a second audience of non-academics, this type of report may well not be effective. Other audiences, such as participants in your research, or clients of a service or innovation you were researching, might best be approached less formally, perhaps by a presentation of some kind or by the production of a short newsletter.

Avoiding Plagiarism

Plagiarism, the passing off of someone else's work as you own, is a hot topic. It is viewed as a serious academic offence, comparable to falsifying or fabricating data. It can result in an otherwise strong project being given a fail grade.

Plagiarism has, in recent years come to the fore due to the easy accessibility of all sorts of material via the Web. You are expected to hunt out relevant material through the Web, printed materials in libraries, suggestions from supervisors or colleagues, or wherever. However, it is crucial that you acknowledge where all such material came from. If you use a quotation (i.e. you copy an exact form of words), this has to be in quotation marks or indented, with an attribution giving where, what and who it came from. The website gives links to sites explaining how this should be done for different types of material.

If you are summarizing material, or taking an idea or finding from any source, you must also say what the source was. You get credit from showing that you have read widely and that what you are saying is in some way linked to, and developing from, what others have done. Obviously a review of previous research which is simply a set of quotations from others, or a list of names of previous researchers and summaries of what they found, is deficient. You need to weave such material into the argument that you are presenting.

Professional Standards

Most course regulations now require word-processed project reports. You are strongly recommended to do this even if it is not a course requirement. A well presented printed report looks professional and almost inevitably influences the reader in your favour. Anyhow, typing and word-processing skills are worth acquiring. Whatever the word limits are, stick to them.

Language matters

There is a tradition, in writing for scientific journals, of adopting a very impersonal language style (past tense, passive voice – 'subjects were asked to . . .'). If your course regulations expect this, then do this, though bear in mind that 'participants' is now preferred to 'subjects' in most disciplines – chapter 5, p. 100. Several reputable journals have now relaxed their rules on language style. If you have greater freedom regulation-wise, then choose a style that you prefer. It is common for reports of flexible design studies to use the active voice and to use the past tense only when describing things that did happen in the past. Look for a report or journal article that reports in a style you think appropriate and use that.

There is general recognition that sexist and racist language is to be avoided in research reports. Apart from the offence that such language can cause, unthinking use of, say, a term such as 'businessman' for both males and females may lead to confusion. Guidelines are available and links are provided on the website.

References

Examiners are likely to treat the quality of your referencing as an index of whether or not your work reaches the required professional standard. There are conventions about referencing that differ from discipline to discipline with the APA (American Psychological Association) style required in several areas of social science research. The website gives links to a range of styles. Check what is expected and make sure that you follow the appropriate model punctiliously.

Obvious defects are where there is a mismatch between references in the text and the list of references at the end. Some in-text references may have been omitted from the list at the end. Or they may differ in some way, perhaps in the dates or the spelling of authors' names. Some in the list may not appear in the text. Sorting this out can be a pain but it just requires time and effort rather than any deep thought. Remember to reference the 'key texts' which you have used repeatedly during the work for the project. They can become so familiar that you forget to include them.

When compiling the reference list you will be very glad that you followed the advice in chapter 3, p. 55, to make sure that you keep full references (names and initials of *all* authors, journal page numbers, etc.) as you come across them. You have let yourself in for a lot of additional hassle if you didn't!

How many references? This is something of a 'how long is a piece of string' question. Don't assume that more is better. Discerning readers (which will include examiners) are going to spot if you are peppering your report with unnecessary references. Relevant previous research should be referenced but, if it's a heavily researched area, you only need to select some good examples. Any claims or assertions should be referenced where feasible. If you reference some specific point with a book or long article, it's good practice to include the relevant page number(s). Don't reference things you have not read. If you can't get hold of something you want to refer to which you find mentioned by someone else, you can cite this as 'Bloggs (2003), as cited in Robinson (2005), claims that . . .'

Look at (successful) project reports and find ones that seem similar to yours. How many references do they have?

Abstracts and executive summaries

An abstract is a short summary of the project, usually included at the beginning of the report. Its exact position and length is likely to be specified in the course regulations which, as always, you disobey at your peril. It should cover what you did, why this is of interest and importance, and what you have found. There is sometimes a requirement to include some key terms giving the main topics covered in the project. A common failing is to describe the project without summarizing the findings.

You can have a go at producing an abstract any time that you are clear about your findings. However, its definitive version is best left as the absolutely final task when writing the report. This abstract should be a polished jewel and it is worth spending time on getting it right. As with other aspects of the report, it often helps to use examples from successful reports as possible models.

It is important because the abstract is probably the first thing that the reader turns to, after noting the project title. Halo effects are almost inevitable. If there are spelling mistakes, clumsy sentences or non-sentences, or anything which gives a negative impression in the mind of the reader, this will colour their approach to the rest of the report. If it impresses positively, you are off to a good start.

The First Full Draft

Completing the first full draft is an important milestone in writing the report. To achieve this, you need to be able to concentrate on writing and not let other tasks get in the way. There may be some additional work to be done in analysis and interpretation arising from the report as you are accumulating the chapters of the report but, with the finishing post in sight, your day-to-day task is writing. Do make sure that you are keeping copies of what you are writing.

Beware the curse of the computer as it prepares a hard disc crash to coincide with your completing the draft!

If you are stuck while writing, you have two choices. One is to keep writing regardless. You might be able to work your way through the block and produce something worthwhile. If you think that what you have produced is pretty awful, mark it in the text as something you are going to have to return to. The alternative when stuck is to tackle some other part of the report. By now, you won't have the luxury of taking a long break and hoping that inspiration will strike.

So, by hook or by crook, you get to the full draft. Inevitably some bits will be worse than others. Don't worry over much about the weaker parts. You can attend to them while revising the draft.

Revising and Polishing

If you can produce a full draft, you are going to finish the project. The next phase, revising and polishing, helps to ensure that you make the most of all your efforts in designing and carrying out the project.

In an ideal world, you would allow a week or two to elapse from completing the draft to trying to revise it. If deadlines loom, it's probably more realistic to think in terms of giving yourself the afternoon off, getting a good sleep and turning to 'revise mode' bright-eyed and bushy-tailed the next morning.

When producing the first draft, you are telling your story of the project; effectively you are writing for yourself. When revising, you need to have the reader, metaphorically, looking over your shoulder as you review what you have written. Would someone else understand what I am getting at here? Do I need to add material so that they can follow the argument?

You also need to polish. Some sentences will be over-long, over-complex and poorly expressed. There will be repetition. You forgot that you had covered something earlier and say it twice. Some repetition is needed to help communication but reference back may be better. Everyone has their favourite words and phrases which they tend to overuse. Find out what yours are (you may have to get a friend to tell you) and seek alternatives. Is the tone right? Are you being condescending to the reader? Or inappropriately friendly? While, traditionally, scientific reports have been written in the rather forbidding linguistic code using passive constructions and the past tense with the voice of the researcher suppressed, you may not be constrained to that extent. Find out the expectations for your report. As ever, you play the game according to the rules set. If there is freedom in the way you can report, then choose whatever style seems to communicate best what you have done and found.

It makes sense to use a spelling checker. If nothing else, it will pick up inadvertent typos where what you have written wasn't what you have intended. I don't like grammar checkers as I spend an inordinate amount of time disagreeing with their suggestions. However, it's up to you. Professional presentation also includes having a standard system for headings and sub-headings in the report and for standard spacing between sections, sub-sections, etc. Find a model you like and follow it. The pages should be numbered and the contents page should give page numbers for the different sections. Check the detailed specifications for the layout and format of all aspects of the report.

The Final Version

Try to get to what you consider the final version a few days (at least) before the deadline for handing it in. Get someone else to proof-read it, i.e. to go through it with a fine-toothed comb looking for any residual things which need tidying up – things like spelling mistakes which a checker doesn't find ('their' when it should be 'there', 'its' for 'it's'), sentences which don't communicate well, etc. At this stage, you don't want someone to be making serious criticisms of the substance of your report as you don't have the time to deal with them. Now is the time to call in a favour from a friend. Use bribery if necessary!

Other Forms of Presentation

Some course regulations call for other presentations of your findings as well as the project report. For example, this might be a short oral presentation in front of some staff and fellow students. This is a valuable exercise, as it is not only the type of thing which anyone following a research or academic career will find they have to do, but it is common in many other graduate job situations.

The key to doing this well is to prepare and to rehearse. Make yourself familiar with PowerPoint and produce a slideshow covering the main points of your project and its findings. Use graphs and figures where possible. Go through it yourself and make sure you can complete it in the time allocated. If at all possible have a dummy run with a few colleagues. Prime them with some good questions that you know the answers to.

On the day, check that you are familiar with the equipment. Remember to face the audience and not just give them your back view. Remember also that your audience can read. You shouldn't spend most of the time just reading out the text on the slides.

Poster presentations are another format widely used at conferences and workshops and for some undergraduate degrees. They call for rather more words than you would use for a slideshow though you may use print-outs of the slides together with additional information. Once again, pay serious attention to the standard of presentation. Some are truly awful.

Some other form of presentation may be needed to fulfil the commitments you made to participants and others, while carrying out the research. This may be in the form of a slide presentation or a short leaflet tailored to the interests and backgrounds of those involved.

A Final Word

If, as suggested in the first chapter, you have got to the end of the book on a first read through, and before you have got in to details of the design and the carrying out of the project, I hope that you feel empowered rather than the reverse. It can seem a daunting prospect but, as with other aspects of life, there comes a time when you have to go for it. So, return to the beginning of the book and get on with the various tasks needed to get it up and running. If your experience is typical, you will find exhilarating periods when you make good progress and others more like wading though treacle. Keep at it.

If you are now getting to the end of the project journey I trust it has worked out well. It can be not only a challenging experience but also a rewarding and enjoyable one. To make only a small contribution to knowledge and understanding is a great thing.

Further Reading

Booth, W. C., Colomb, G. G. and Williams, J. M. (2003) *The Craft of Research.* 2nd edition. Chicago: University of Chicago Press. Should be required reading for anyone wanting to produce a professional standard report. Blend of wisdom and practical tips.

Chapter 7 Tasks

1 Find out what your course regulations say about the report and its presentation. This includes aspects such as the format and structure, the referencing system to be used, the length (and whether appendices are to be included in the word count – they usually are not counted) and the deadline date for submission of the report.

2 Find out whether the supervisor will comment on a draft of the report. Practices vary on this. If supervisors will comment, make sure you take this opportunity and take serious note of any comments or suggestions. Let them have the draft in time for them to read it and for you to act on suggestions before the deadline. It is better to let them have an incomplete draft, in time for comments, than to submit a finished version which leaves insufficient time. Now that you have gone through all the chapters, I hope that you have an appreciation of the main things to sort out in designing and delivering a quality project.

If you haven't already done so, now is a good time to have a go at the tasks listed in the previous chapters. They are best tackled following, more or less, the sequence in the book and before you get yourself into the main data collection phase.

References and Author Index

The list of references incorporates an author index. The numbers in **bold** at the end of each entry indicate where the publication is referred to in this book.

Adamson, L. and Meister, D. G. (2005) Teachers' knowledge about adolescents: An interview study. *Scandinavian Journal of Psychology*, 46, 343–8. **55**

Barzun, J. and Graff, H. F. (2000) *The Modern Researcher*. 6th edition. Belmont, CA: Wadsworth. **29**

Booth, W. C., Colomb, G. G. and Williams, J. M. (2003) *The Craft of Research*. 2nd edition. Chicago: University of Chicago Press. **2, 12, 142, 144**

Coolican, H. (2004) *Research Methods and Statistics in Psychology*. 4th edition. London: Hodder Education. **53**

Craig, G., Corden, A. and Thornton, P. (2000) Safety in social research. *Social Research Update* Issue 20. Department of Sociology, University of Surrey. (www.soc.surrey.ac.uk/sru/SRU29.html) **104**

Cresswell, J. W. (2003) *Research Design: Qualitative, quantitative and mixed method approaches*. 2nd edition. London and Thousand Oaks, CA: Sage. **22**

Danermark, B., Ekström, M., Jakobsen, L. and Karlsson, J. C. (2002) *Explaining Society: Critical realism in the social sciences*. London: Routledge. **135**

Dunbar, G. (2005) *Evaluating Research Methods in Psychology: A case study approach*. Oxford: Blackwell Publishing. **48**

Glaser, B. and Strauss, A. (1967) *The Discovery of Grounded Theory*. Chicago: Aldine Press. **39**

Hakim, C. (1987) *Research Design: Successful designs for social economic research*. London: Routledge. **21**

Matthieson, S. B., Aasen, E., Holst, G., Wie, K. and Ståle, E. (2003) The escalation of conflict: a case study of bullying at work. *International Journal of Management and Decision Making*, 4, 96–112. **55**

OECD [Organization for Economic Cooperation and Development] (2004)

Equity in Education: Students with disabilities, learning difficulties and disadvantages. Paris: OECD. **135**

Pawson, R. and Tilley, N. (1997) Realistic Evaluation. London and Thousand Oaks, CA: Sage. **20, 136**

Robson, C. (1994) Experiment, Design and Statistics in Psychology. 3rd edition. Harmondsworth: Penguin (available at www.blackwellpublishing.com/robson/ebook.htm). **124**

Robson, C. (2000) Small-Scale Evaluation: Principles and practice. London and Thousand Oaks, CA: Sage. **11**

Robson, C. (2002) Real World Research: A resource for social-scientists and practitioner-researchers. 2nd edition. Oxford: Blackwell Publishing. **92**

Scott, J. (1990) A Matter of Record: Documentary sources in social research. Cambridge: Polity Press. **89**

Strauss, A. and Corbin, J. (1998) Basics of Qualitative Research: Techniques and procedures for developing grounded theory. 2nd edition. London and Thousand Oaks, CA: Sage. **39**

Sylva, K., Melhuish, E. C., Sammons, P., Siraj-Blatchford, I. and Taggart, B. (2004) The Effective Provision of Pre-school Education (EPPE) Project: Technical paper 12 – the final report. London: DfES/Institute of Education, University of London. **143**

Subject Index

abstract: in project report, 148
access: field research, 100
action research, 23: advantages and disadvantages of, 5
alternative hypotheses, 53
analysis: discourse, 45: narrative, 45
analysis of data, 115: preparing for, 116
analysis of documents, 28
analysis of variance, 128
arguments (research arguments), 72
arithmetic mean, 123
audience (considering your audience), 9, 145
audio taping of interviews, 107
authenticity of a document, 90
avoidance of sexist and racist language, 147

bar chart, 119, 125
bibliographic software, 64

case studies, 26: advantages and disadvantages of, 27
categorical data (variables), 117: summarizing and displaying, 119
census, 41
central tendency, 123
Chi-square, 122, 128
clinical significance, 127
cluster sample, 99
Cochran Q test, 128

coding of qualitative (non-numerical) data, 131
coding (in grounded theory study): open, 133; selective, 133; theoretical, 133
Cohen's d, 126
collaboration, 16
confidence interval, 124, 126
confidentiality, 103
constructive replication, 50
continuous variables, 122: displaying, 125
contracts (formal and informal), 103
correlation coefficient, 127: Pearson product-moment, 127, 128
course regulations, 7: need to conform to, 47, 152
credibility, 71: of a document, 90
cross-classification (cross-tabulation), 120

data (plural or singular?), 14
data analysis, 115: preparing for, 116
data collection, 13, 106: choice of method, 92; dealing with disaster, 108; design difficulties, 108; difficulties in completing, 107; need for plan B, 107, 109; practicalities, 97; selecting method of, 70
Data Protection Act, 65
data reduction and organization (qualitative data), 130

data: interpretation of, 135; reliability of, 71; validity of, 72; verbal, 130
deception, 67, 100
demands on the researcher (of different approaches), 23
dependent variable, 36
depth interviews, 75
design of research, 21, 51: development of, 53; fixed, 22; flexible, 22
diaries: as data collection method, 80, 81; research or project diary, 16
discourse analysis, 45
discussion groups (web based), 12, 61
documentary analysis, 28, 88: advantages and disadvantages of, 89
documents: trustworthiness of, 29; assessing data quality, 89; using documents, 88, 91

effect sizes, 126
EndNote, 64
ethical issues, 2, 64: avoiding the unethical, 66; guidelines, 66; problems in field research, 103; research involving vulnerable groups, 67; use of deception, 67
ethics approval document, 65
ethics committees, 65
ethnographic approach, 30; advantages and disadvantages of, 32; ethnographic-style research, 30
evaluation research, 32: advantages and disadvantages of, 34; purposes of, 33
exact replication (of research), 50
Excel, 119, 124
executive summaries, 148
experiments, 35: advantages and disadvantages of, 38; multiple base-line design, 38; need for pre-knowledge, 137; quasi-experiments, 37; single-case (single-subject) design, 37; true experiment, 36

feasibility (of research project), 2, 47
feminist research, 44
field research: access for, 100; ethical problems in, 103

fixed designs, 22: example of project schedule, 110
flexible designs, 22: example of project schedule, 111
focus groups, 76
formal and informal contracts, 103
formal approval, obtaining, 102
frequency counts, 121
Friedman test, 128
fully structured interviews, 73

Gantt charts, 109
Google, 56
Google Scholar, 56
grounded theory studies, 39: advantages and disadvantages of, 40; approach to analysis, 132
group interviews, 76: focus groups, 76
group projects, 10: working together successfully, 12

help (getting help), 7
hermeneutic research, 44
histogram, 125
hypotheses, 53
hypothetico-deductive approach, 53

independent variable, 36
individual research, 10
informal interviews, 76
informed consent, 100, 102
insider research, 104: difficulties, 104; ethical issues, 104
internet searching, 56
inter-observer reliability, 71
interpretation of data, 135
inter-quartile range, 124
interviews, 73: advantages and disadvantages of, 77; audio taping of, 107; depth interviews, 75; focus groups, 76; fully structured, 73; group, 76; informal, 76; semi-structured, 74; telephone interviews, 77; transcripts of, 75; unstructured, 75; using in your project, 78
Intute, 56

Intute Virtual Training Suite, 56: example of material from, 57

key word searching, 55
Kruskal-Wallis test, 128

laboratory research, 100
library research, 90
library searching (for sources), 61
listservs, 61
literature review, 54

Mann-Whitney test, 128
McNemar test, 128
mean (arithmetic), 123
meaning of a document, 90
mechanisms, 20, 135, 144
median, 124
memoing, 131
method of data collection, 70: choice of, 92
method triangulation, 26, 70
milestones (for the project), 13
mini-ethnographies, 30
multiple base-line design, 38
multiple methods, use of, 92
multiple regression analysis, 128

narrative analysis, 45
non-parametric tests, 126
non-probability samples, 99
normal distribution, 124
note making, 63
NUD·IST, 133
null hypotheses, 53
NVivo, 133

observation: participant, 85; structured, 84; using in your project, 86
on-line research, 92
open coding, 133
ordered categorical variables, 118
outliers, 124

participant observation, 30, 85: advantages and disadvantages of, 87
participants (not subjects), 100, 147

Pearson product-moment correlation, 127
phenomenological research, 44
pilot studies, 105
plagiarism, 146
plan B in data collection, 107, 109
poster presentations, 150
practitioner researchers: constraints on research topic, 49
primary sources, 88
ProCite, 64
project diary, 16
project milestones, 13
project planning checklist, 5
project reports: abstracts and executive summaries, 148; alternative forms of presentation, 150; avoidance of sexist and racist language, 147; final version, 150; first full draft, 148; language style, 147; need for professional standards, 146; poster presentations, 159; revising and polishing, 149
project schedule, 109: example for fixed design project, 110; example for flexible design project, 111
purposive samples, 99

qualitative (non-numerical) data: analysis, 130; coding, 131; conceptualizing, 132; data reduction and organization, 130; displaying, 132; editing, 131; grounded theory approach to analysis, 132; memoing, 131; summarizing, 131; use of computer packages for analysis, 133
qualitative/quantitative divide, the, 21
quasi-experimental designs, 37
questionnaires, 79: advantages and disadvantages of, 81; design of, 79; using in your project, 81
quota samples, 99

random sample, 98: selecting, 98
randomized controlled trial (RCT), 36
range, 123; semi-inter-quartile range, 124
reading skills, 63
realism, 135

reference managers, 64
references: need for full references, 55; number of, 147; quality of referencing, 147; referencing styles, 147
reliability, 71: inter-observer, 71
replication research, 50
report writing, 13, 137
reports: planning and drafting, 140; structure of, 141
representative samples, 98
representativeness: of a document, 90
research approach: choosing an approach, 44
research arguments, 72, 142: claims, 143; reasons and evidence, 143
research design, 21, 51: development of, 53
research diary, 16
research focus, 13
research purpose, 19: descriptive purpose, 19; emancipatory purpose, 20; explanatory purpose, 20; exploratory purpose, 20
research questions, 13: examples of, 51; need for, 52; selection of, 50
research strategy (style), 13
research topic, 13; avoidance of sensitive, 48; examples of, 48; feasibility of, 47; selection of, 47; topics to avoid, 48
researcher risks in field research, 104
researcher safety in field research, 104

samples: sizes, 97; cluster, 99; non-probability, 99; purposive, 99; quota, 99; random, 98; representative sampling, 98; selecting a random sample, 98; stratified, 99; survey sampling, 41; theoretical, 99
satisfaction ratings: analysis of, 118
scales, 82: advantages and disadvantages of, 83; using in your project, 83
scatter plot, 127, 129
searching: asking the author, 62; internet, 56; library-based, 61
secondary data, 88
secondary sources, 88
selective coding, 133

semi-inter-quartile range, 124
semi-structured interviews, 74
sensitive topics: avoidance of, 48
significance: clinical, 127; statistical, 125
single-case (single-subject) design, 37
skills provided by doing a project, 9
Social Sciences Internet Gateway (SOSIG), 56
sources: dealing with, 62; finding and using, 54; keeping a record of, 63; planning the search for, 55; primary sources, 88; secondary sources, 88; tertiary sources, 88; using the internet to search for, 56
standard deviation, 123
Statistical Package for the Social Sciences (SPSS), 122, 124, 127
statistical significance, 125
statistical tests, 125: choice of, 127, 128; non-parametric, 126; t-test, 126, 128
statistics: summary (descriptive), 123, 129
stratified sample, 99
structured observation, 84: advantages and disadvantages of, 84
subjects (participants), 100
summary (descriptive) statistics, 123, 129
supervisors: expectations, 7; support, 11
support groups, 11, 103
surveys, 41: advantages and disadvantages of, 43; design, 42; response rates, 41

telephone interviews, 77
tertiary sources, 88
tests and scales, 82: advantages and disadvantages of, 83; using in your project, 83
tests: statistical, 125; choice of, 127; non-parametric, 126; t-test, 126, 128
theoretical coding, 133
theoretical sampling, 99
topic: selection of, 47
triangulation, 26: of methods, 70
true experiment, 36
trustworthiness, 71: of documents, 29
t-test, 126, 128

unobtrusive measures, 90
unstructured interviews, 75

validity, 72
variability (spread): calculating, 124;
   measures of (range, standard
   deviation, variance), 123
variables, 35: categorical, 117;
   continuous, 122; dependent variable,
   36; displaying continuous variables,

125; independent variable, 36; ordered
   categorical, 118
variance, 123
verbal data, 130
vulnerable groups: use in research, 67

web-based discussion groups, 12, 61
Wilcoxon test, 128
worthwhile projects: for participants, 9;
   for yourself, 8